I R I S H
PASSENGER LISTS
1803 – 1806

IRISH
PASSENGER LISTS
1803 – 1806

Lists of Passengers Sailing from
Ireland to America
EXTRACTED FROM THE HARDWICKE PAPERS

REFERENCE
Compiled under the Editorial Supervision of
BRIAN MITCHELL

Copyright © 1995
Genealogical Publishing Co., Inc.
1001 N. Calvert St., Baltimore, MD 21202
Library of Congress Catalogue Card Number 94-79986
International Standard Book Number 0-8063-1458-3
Made in the United States of America

The Hardwicke Papers

No official registers of passengers leaving Irish ports were ever kept except for the brief period from March 1803 to March 1806 inclusive. Masters of ships were required by law to "comply in every respect with the Act for regulating the carrying of Passengers 43rd. of King George the 3rd. of the United Kingdom of Great Britain and Ireland."

For this brief period lists of emigrants to the United States are contained within the so-called Hardwicke Papers (now held in the British Library, London). These lists with particulars of age, occupation and, in most cases, place of abode were compiled by the masters of emigrant ships and were sworn before the Commissioner, a Customs official, in the Custom House of the port from which the ships were to sail.

A duplicate of these oaths was then submitted to the Lord Lieutenant of Ireland. The Lord Lieutenant's permission was required before any emigrant ship could leave port. Earl Hardwicke was Lord Lieutenant of Ireland from 1801 to 1806.

The date that heads each list refers to the day an Order of Council was granted giving permission for a ship to sail. It does not refer to the actual date the ship sailed, although in most cases, weather permitting, the ship would have sailed shortly after the granting of the Order of Council.

At this time the Government was largely hostile to emigration and especially to the emigration of skilled tradesmen and craftsmen such as linen weavers. The ship's captain had to swear that to "the best of his knowledge" none of his passengers "is or are artificers, artisans, manufacturers, seamen or seafaring men."

Permission, for example, was denied for six of the Numa's passengers to emigrate from the port of Limerick to Charleston in March 1803 because they were deemed to be skilled craftsmen.

For the Government's purpose the occupations of intending emigrants was the most crucial piece of information in the Hardwicke Papers. For family historians today the most useful piece of information is the identification, in many cases, of the emigrant's place of residence in Ireland.

Since they were compiled in the early 1800s, the Hardwicke Papers predate the so-called customs passenger lists which record the arrival of immigrants at American ports from 1820. The Hardwicke lists are, therefore, priceless since, in many cases, they will be the only surviving record of an ancestor's emigration to the States.

Altogether, 109 sailings from Irish ports are recorded in the Hardwicke Papers with the breakdown as follows: Dublin 28; Londonderry 26; Belfast 22; Newry 19; Sligo 6; Warrenpoint 3; Cork 2; Ballyshannon 1; Killybegs 1; and Limerick 1. The three major northern ports of Belfast, Londonderry and Newry accounted for 61% of sailings (67 in total) in this period. These lists record 35 sailings in 1803; 37 in 1804; 29 in 1805; and 8 in 1806 (the lists end in March 1806).

All ships recorded in the Hardwicke lists were destined for the United States. New York was by far the most popular destination with 66 (61%) arrivals. The Philadelphia/Newcastle/Wilmington area accounted for 24 (22%); Baltimore 7; Boston 4; Charleston 4; New Bedford 1; Norfolk 1; Wiscasset 1; and unspecified port 1.

Be careful when interpreting the Irish place names recorded in these lists. Place names have been spelled as they appear in the records. For example, Drumarra refers to Dromara, County Down; NewtownLimavady is better known today as Limavady, County Londonderry; Lowtherstown as Irvinestown, County Fermanagh; Queen's County refers to the present-day county of Leix and King's County to Offaly. Use books such as *A New Genalogical Atlas of Ireland* and the *Townland Index* to identify places recorded in this book. It must always be remembered that standardization in the spelling of surnames and place names in Ireland is only a phenomenon of the 20th century. In some cases local knowledge within a specific district in Ireland (in this case the area around the port from which the emigrant left) may well be needed to decipher place names. In most cases, however, common sense and a good reference book will be all the assistance required in identifying the residences listed in this book.

Acknowledgements

Many thanks to the employees of the Genealogy Centre and Typing Pool who extracted, checked, computerized, tabulated and produced these lists into their finished format. All are on the staff of the Inner City Trust, Londonderry. Funding of the project was made possible by the Northern Ireland Training and Employment Agency (under their Action for Community Employment programme).

I am grateful to the British Library Board, London, for granting permission to publish these lists.

Brian Mitchell

Sailings Recorded in
The Hardwicke Papers

No.	Date	Destination	Departure
1	March 1803	America	Dublin
2		Charleston	Limerick
3		New York	Belfast
4	April 1803	New York	Dublin
5		Newcastle & Philadelphia	Warrenpoint
6		New York	Sligo
7		New York	Newry
8		Philadelphia	Belfast
9		Wilmington & Philadelphia	Londonderry
10		New York	Londonderry
11		New York	Londonderry
12		Philadelphia	Londonderry
13		Baltimore	Londonderry
14		New York	Sligo
15	May 1803	Baltimore	Londonderry
16		Philadelphia	Londonderry
17		Philadelphia	Warrenpoint
18		Philadelphia	Newry
19		New York	Newry
20	June 1803	New York	Newry
21	July 1803	New York	Belfast
22		Wiscasset, U.S.A.	Dublin
23	August 1803	New York	Dublin
24		New York	Dublin
25		New York	Belfast
26		New York	Dublin
27	September 1803	New York	Dublin
28		New York	Cork
29		New York	Londonderry
30		New York	Dublin

31		Philadelphia	Belfast
32		New York	Newry
33		Charleston	Belfast
34	November 1803	New York	Londonderry
35		Norfolk, U.S.A.	Dublin
36	February 1804	New York	Cork
37		New York	Belfast
38	March 1804	Philadelphia	Dublin
39		New York	Belfast
40		Philadelphia	Londonderry
41	April 1804	New York	Sligo
42		New York	Londonderry
43		Wilmington	Newry
44		New York	Sligo
45		New York	Dublin
46		Philadelphia	Londonderry
47		Baltimore	Belfast
48		New York	Belfast
49		New York	Dublin
50		Philadelphia	Dublin
51	May 1804	Newcastle	Newry
52		Philadelphia	Belfast
53		New York	Dublin
54		Baltimore	Londonderry
55		New York	Newry
56		Newcastle & Philadelphia	Ballyshannon
57		New York	Londonderry
58		Baltimore	Dublin
59		New York	Londonderry
60	June 1804	New York	Newry
61		New York	Londonderry
62		Newcastle & Philadelphia	Killybegs
63		Boston	Dublin
64	August 1804	New York	Belfast
65		Charleston	Belfast
66		New York	Londonderry
67	September 1804	New York	Dublin
68		New York	Belfast
69		Boston	Belfast
70		New York	Dublin

71		New York	Dublin
72	October 1804	New York	Newry
73	February 1805	New York	Dublin
74	March 1805	New York	Belfast
75		New York	Londonderry
76	April 1805	New York	Belfast
77		New York	Dublin
78		New York	Dublin
79		New York	Sligo
80		Philadelphia	Londonderry
81		New York	Londonderry
82		New York	Londonderry
83	May 1805	New Bedford	Newry
84		Baltimore	Londonderry
85		New York	Newry
86		Newcastle & Philadelphia	Warrenpoint
87		Philadelphia	Newry
88		Boston	Newry
89		New York	Newry
90	June 1805	New York	Newry
91		Philadelphia	Londonderry
92	July 1805	New York	Dublin
93		New York	Belfast
94		Newcastle & Philadelphia	Londonderry
95		Philadelphia	Newry
96	August 1805	New York	Belfast
97		Boston	Dublin
98	September 1805	Charleston	Belfast
99		New York	Sligo
100	October 1805	New York	Dublin
101	November 1805	New York	Belfast
102	February 1806	New York	Dublin
103		New York	Newry
104		New York	Belfast
105		Baltimore	Londonderry
106	March 1806	New York	Newry
107		Philadelphia	Dublin
108		New York	Dublin
109		New York	Londonderry

IRISH
PASSENGER LISTS
1803 – 1806

SHIP:	MARS	TO:	America
SAIL DATE: 29 March 1803		FROM:	Dublin

NAME	AGE	OCCUPATION	RESIDENCE
FORD, William		Gentleman	
MORRIS, John		Servant	
SHERLOCK, William		Merchant	
JACKSON, Hugh		Merchant	
GIBSON, Robert		American Merchant	
TEELING, ?		Clerk	
MURPHY, James		Labourer	
HOBLETON, John		Labourer	

1

SHIP:	NUMA		TO:	Charlestown

SHIP: NUMA   TO: Charlestown

SAIL DATE: 29 March 1803   FROM: Limerick

NAME	AGE	OCCUPATION	RESIDENCE
ADAMS, Charles	48	Farmer	Limerick
ADAMS, Margaret	39		Limerick
O'CARROLL, Richard	22	Farmer	Dolinbroke
O'CARROLL, Daniel	20	Farmer	Dolinbroke
EGAN, Thomas	29	Writing Clerk	Limerick
CORRY, Martin	58	Labourer	Limerick
CONNERY, John	29	Labourer	Limerick
EGAN, Mary	60		Limerick
CORRY, Eliza	33		Limerick
CONNORY, Mary	26		Limerick
EGAN, Mary Jun	27		Limerick
FITZPATRICK, Betty	56		Limerick
QUILLAN, Michael	48	Gentleman	Limerick
QUINLAN, Mary	46		Limerick
QUINLAN, Mary Jun	13		Limerick
O'DWYER, Thomas	22	Gentleman	Limerick
O'DONNOVAN, Michael	26	Gentleman	Limerick
MULLINS, John	26	Labourer	Limerick
MEEHAN, James	26	Labourer	Clare
KERNAN, Patrick	24	Labourer	Clare
MURRAY, Terence	18	Labourer	Clare
MAGRATH, Patrick	21	Labourer	Clare
LEE, Andrew	26	Labourer	Caperass
CONNERY, Richard	19	Writing Clerk	Limerick
MORGAN, Hugh	22	Labourer	Limerick
KERLY, James	37	Farmer	Ballyhoben
WALSH, John	27	Labourer	Limerick
CONSIDEN, Ann	22		Limerick
CUMMINS, John	21	Labourer	Claraline, Co Tipperary
O'BRIEN, William	26	Labourer	Thomastown
FEHILLY, Margaret	24		Limerick
HAYES, Margaret	18		Limerick
CALLAGHAN, Mary	14		Limerick
FEHILLY, Joseph	7		Limerick
FEHILLY, Michael	5		Limerick
FEHILLY, John	3		Limerick
FEHILLY, Mary	2		Limerick
NOT PERMITTED TO EMIGRATE			
RYAN, Thomas			
CRONNAN, John			
DALY, John			
RYAN, Patrick			
ENRIGHT, Michael			
HENNESY, Patrick			

NAME	AGE	OCCUPATION	RESIDENCE
RADCLIFFE, Alexander	23	Farmer	Ballyroney
HUNTER, John	28	Labourer	Belfast
CALVERT, Will	33	Labourer	Killeagh
CALVERT, Ann	24	Spinster	Killeagh
BRYSON, James	27	Farmer	Kilrock
LEONARD, Peter	28	Farmer	Hillsboro
LOGAN, Will	36	Labourer	Dromore
BAIN, Thomas	18	Farmer	Downpatrick
WEBB, Joseph	25	Labourer	Cockslem
WILSON, William	22	Labourer	Derrylea
WILSON, Margaret	20	Spinster	Derrylea
KINCARD, William	52	Farmer	Derrylea
KINCARD, Robert	18	Labourer	Derrylea
HANCOCK, William	19	Labourer	Derrylea
WILSON, Thomas	23	Labourer	Armagh
DRENNAN, James	19	Labourer	Cavehill
ENGLISH, John	40	Labourer	Tynan
ENGLISH, Isabella	32		Tynan
KERR, William	18	Labourer	Tynan
LYSTER, George	25	Labourer	Tynan
LISTER, James	20	Labourer	Tynan
GRAHAM, John	24	Labourer	Tynan
SPRATT, Thomas	50	Farmer	Clough
BROWN, John	24	Farmer	Saintfield
CAMPBELL, Samuel	18	Labourer	Banbridge
MARTIN, Charles	20	Farmer	Ballynahinch
HALBRIDGE, Robert	16	Clerk	Ballymoney
EAKIN, Robert	38	Farmer	Coleraine
RAFIELD, William	23	Farmer	Ballymena
WOODS, William	27	Labourer	Sea Patrick
KIDD, Archibald	20	Labourer	Keady
SHIELDS, John	20	Farmer	Keady
CULLY, John	24	Farmer	Keady
CLEMENTS, David	22	Farmer	Keady
CLEMENTS, Andrew	20	Farmer	Keady
McALISTER, William	20	Farmer	Ballycaster

SHIP:	SUSAN		TO:	New York
SAIL DATE:	5 April 1803		FROM:	Dublin

NAME	AGE	OCCUPATION	RESIDENCE
CONKLIN, John	25	Master	New York
DAVIS, James	26	Mate	Rhode Island
SMITH, Andrew	34	Boatsvain	Jermainestown, Delaware
HOWADD, Thomas	29	Seaman	New York
BURGIS, John	32	Seaman	State of New York
CHAPPLE, Anthony	23	Seaman	State of New Jersey
CUMP, John	27	Seaman	Germainestown
SMITH, John	36	Seaman	State of Maryland
BERHAM, Silas	21	Seaman	State of Connecticut
PATTERSON, George	40		State of Connecticut
DORNAN, John	43	Bookseller	Dublin
DORNAN, Mary (Mrs)	40		Dublin
Three Small Children			
RUSSEL, Frances (Mrs)	40	Grocer	Dublin
RUSSEL, Anna (Mrs)	38	Spinster	Louth
Three Small Children			
MIDLETON, John	29	Merchant	Louth
ERWIN, James	28	Physician	Louth
ERWIN, William	26	Physician	Louth
RIVINGTON, Charles	25	Merchant	New York
NOBLE, Robert	60	Merchant	New York
WELCH, Nelly (Mrs)	31	Spinster	(Ireland/Wexford)
FINLY, Mary Ann (Miss)	21	Spinster	Meath
TRUER, James	22	Farmer	Co of Meath
FITZGERALD, Thomas	23	Farmer	Co of Meath
BYRNE, James	19	Farmer	Co of Meath
BYRNE, John	21	Farmer	Co of Meath
FINLY, William	18	Farmer	Co of Wexford
KELLY, James	24	Farmer	Co of Wexford
KELLY, William	29	Farmer	Co of Wexford
RILEY, John	31	Farmer	Co of Wexford
KELLY, James	25	Farmer	Co of Wexford

SHIP:	NEPTUNE		TO:	Newcastle & Philadelphia
SAIL DATE:	12 April 1803		FROM:	Warrenpoint

NAME	AGE	OCCUPATION	RESIDENCE
GRIMES, John	28	Labourer	
GRIMES, Agnes	26		
CRUMMY, James	45	Farmer	
CRUMMY, Agnes	30		
CRUMMY, Mary	15		
CRUMMY, Sarah	12		
CRUMMY, James	6		
CRUMMY, David	4		
DINE, Susan	18	Spinster	
GALLON, David	40	Farmer	
HENRY, John	40	Farmer	
HENRY, Hanna	30		
HENRY, Nancy	13		
HENRY, James	11		
COUNTER, William	26	Labourer	
COUNTER, Mary	25		

NAME	AGE	OCCUPATION	RESIDENCE
SHIP:		RACHEL	TO: New York
SAIL DATE: 19 April 1803			FROM: Sligo

NAME	AGE	OCCUPATION	RESIDENCE
ORMSBY, Robert		Clerk	
GILLAN, James		Farmer	
READ, John		Clerk	
HENDERSON, James		Clerk	
McGOWAN, Peter		Schoolmaster	
ARMSTRONG, Charles		Clerk	
CHRISTIAN, Laurence		Labourer	
CHRISTIAN, Patt		Labourer	
DONALD, James		Labourer	
CORRY, William		Labourer	
McGOWAN, Daniel		Labourer	
McGOWAN, Owen		Labourer	
CORRY, Frederick		Labourer	
GILMARTIN, Pat		Labourer	
GILAN, Pat		Labourer	
FOLEY, Pat		Labourer	
FEENY, Pat		Labourer	
HORAN, Michael		Labourer	
FARREL, John		Labourer	
COMMINS, John		Labourer	
GILMARTIN, Daniel		Labourer	

SHIP:	MAGNET	TO:	New York
SAIL DATE:	19 April 1803	FROM:	Newry

NAME	AGE	OCCUPATION	RESIDENCE
BROTHERS, Elizabeth	44		
BROTHERS, Mary	19		
BROTHERS, Samuel	12	Labourer	
BROTHERS, James	10		
BROTHERS, William	7		
ANDERSON, M Ann	30		
DOUBTY, Mathew	12		
FARRELL, James	30	Labourer	
FARRELL, Elizabeth	22		
FARRELL, William	3		
HARKNESS, James	40	Labourer	
HARKNESS, Jane	36		
HARKNESS, Thomas	12		
HARKNESS, Margaret	10		
HARKNESS, Sarah	10		
HARKNESS, Abigail	8		
HARKNESS, Robert	6		
HARKNESS, James	4		
STORY, Elizabeth	47		
STORY, Ben	18	Farmer	
STORY, Ann	16		
ALEXANDER, Hugh	29	Labourer	
ALEXANDER, Jane	22		
ALEXANDER, Jane	3		
ALEXANDER, Sarah	2		
GOOEY, Robert	20	Farmer	
DOUGLAS, Samuel	18	Farmer	
HARTEN, Thomas	19	Labourer	
ROLSTON, John	27	Labourer	
BEARD, Ann	24		
BEARD, Ann	2		
McCLEAN, James	60	Farmer	
McCLEAN, Elizabeth	60		
McCLEAN, David	24	Labourer	
McCLEAN, John	22	Labourer	
McCLEAN, George	28	Labourer	
RIDDLE, William	19	Labourer	
MAGIL, Samuel	21	Labourer	
MAGIL, Samuel	39	Labourer	
ENERY, Biddy	35	Labourer	

SHIP:	EDWARD		TO:	Philadelphia
SAIL DATE:	19 April 1803		FROM:	Belfast

NAME	AGE	OCCUPATION	RESIDENCE
GREG, James	46	Farmer	
GREG, Thomas	18	Farmer	
GREG, John	19	Farmer	
FLEMING, Thomas	19	Labourer	
PORTER, Hugh	24	Labourer	
MARTIN, John	21	Labourer	
McMEIKIN, Alexander	21	Labourer	
DUNN, William	30	Farmer	
MONKS, Thomas	60	Farmer	
MONKS, Robert	22	Farmer	
MONKS, Joseph	20	Farmer	
MONKS, Thomas	17	Farmer	
SMITH, John	20	Labourer	
McBRIDE, Hugh	26	Labourer	
McBRIDE, W	25	Labourer	
DAWSON, W	28	Labourer	
CRAVEN, John	25	Labourer	
FOX, James	40	Labourer	
MOONEY, Patrick	16	Labourer	
TORVEL, James	22	Labourer	
BURNS, James	20	Labourer	
LABODY, Robert	32	Gentleman	
McCULLOGH, Hers	27	Farmer	
SCOTT, William	22	Farmer	
KIRKMAN, James	40	Farmer	
BINGHAM, William	40	Farmer	
BINGHAM, James	14	Farmer	
NORRIS, John	16	Labourer	
MURPHY, Hugh	18	Labourer	
WILSON, Edward	18	Gentleman	
HANLAY, Aadsal	24	Labourer	
READ, James	23	Labourer	
HADDOCK, Joseph	27	Labourer	

SHIP:	PENSYLVANIA	TO:	Newcastle, Wilmington and Philadelphia
SAIL DATE:	19 April 1803	FROM:	Londonderry

NAME	AGE	OCCUPATION	RESIDENCE
LEALER, Patrick	50	Labourer	Strabane
DONALDSON, Robert	46	Labourer	Strabane
DONALDSON, Bell	36	Spinster	Strabane
DONALDSON, Mary	24	Spinster	Strabane
DONALDSON, Jane	25	Spinster	Strabane
DONALDSON, Mary	20	Spinster	Claudy
MAXWELL, Nancy	30	Spinster	Claudy
MAXWELL, Robert	10	Labourer	Claudy
DONALD, Nathaniel	26	Labourer	Claudy
DONAL, Patrick	50	Labourer	Claudy
STEELE, Margaret	26	Spinster	Claudy
DERIN, Peter	56	Labourer	Claudy
McGONAGAL, James	26	Labourer	Tubermore
CANNEY, Charles	28	Labourer	Tubermore
DOUGHERTY, Richard	36	Labourer	Tubermore
HEATON, Margaret	28	Spinster	Tubermore
McCALLEN, Patrick	33	Labourer	Tubermore
BREESON, Hugh	36	Labourer	Tubermore
O'DONNELL, Denis	40	Labourer	Tubermore
O'DONNELL, Mary	25	Spinster	Strabane
GILMOUR, Samuel	20		St Johnston
GILMOUR, Ann	15	Spinster	St Johnston
ELGIN, James	10	Labourer	St Johnston
BOYD, James	26	Labourer	St Johnston
OLIVER, William	26	Labourer	St Johnston
WILSON, Thomas	25	Labourer	St Johnston
WILSON, Nancy	26	Spinster	St Johnston
WILSON, Nancy Jun	24	Spinster	St Johnston
WILSON, James	20	Labourer	Muff
WILSON, John	56	Labourer	Muff
WILSON, James	45	Labourer	Muff
WILSON, Eleanor	36	Spinster	Newton Limavady
MOORE, John	22	Farmer	Newton Limavady
DEVER, Bridget	55	Spinster	Newton Limavady
LEWIS, John	33	Labourer	Newton Limavady
LEWIS, Fanny	70	Spinster	Newton Limavady
LEWIS, Fanny Jun	15	Spinster	Newton Limavady
LEWIS, Andrew	20	Labourer	Newton Limavady
LEWIS, Susan	36	Spinster	Newton Limavady
LEWIS, George	33	Labourer	Newton Limavady
STEWART, James	25	Labourer	Dungiven
KING, James	45	Labourer	Dungiven
McBRIDE, William	50	Labourer	Dungiven
PARKER, William	61	Labourer	Dungiven
HOUSTON, Alexander	45	Labourer	Dungiven
HOUSTON, Francis	20	Labourer	Dungiven
BRINGHAM, John	26	Farmer	Dungiven
BRINGHAM, Jane	25	Spinster	Ballyshannon
BRINGHAM, Elizabeth	26	Spinster	Ballyshannon
BRINGHAM, Ezekiel	25	Labourer	Ballyshannon
BRINGHAM, David	22	Labourer	Ballyshannon
WHITE, William	18	Labourer	Ballyshannon
MITCHELL, James	22	Labourer	Derry
DERMOT, Thomas	20	Labourer	Derry
MONTGOMERY, William	22	Labourer	Derry
MONTGOMERY, Margaret	41	Spinster	Derry
MONTGOMERY, Samuel	26	Labourer	Derry
MONTGOMERY, Margaret	31	Spinster	Derry
MONTGOMERY, Samuel	12	Labourer	Derry·
MONTGOMERY, Rebecca	10	Spinster	Ballindreat
LITTLE, Robert	26	Labourer	Ballindreat
LITTLE, John	24	Labourer	Ballindreat

SHIP:	PENSYLVANIA	TO:	Newcastle, Wilmington and Philadelphia
SAIL DATE: 19 April 1803		FROM: Londonderry	

NAME	AGE	OCCUPATION	RESIDENCE
ARMSTRONG, Mathew	23	Labourer	Ballindreat
TODD, James	20	Labourer	Ballindreat

SHIP:	CORNELIA	TO:	New York
SAIL DATE:	19 April 1803	FROM:	Londonderry

NAME	AGE	OCCUPATION	RESIDENCE
LITTLE, Andrew	35	Labourer	
LITTLE, Jane	26	Spinster	
LITTLE, John	12	Labourer	
LITTLE, Margaret	9	Spinster	
LITTLE, William	6	A Child	
LITTLE, Eliza	4	A Child	
LITTLE, Jane	2	A Child	
McAVENY, Hugh	24	Farmer	
McAVENY, Jane	30	Spinster	
McAVENY, Jane	1	A Child	
NEILSON, Simon	25	Labourer	
NEILSON, Mary	25	Spinster	
ARMSTRONG, Archibald	18	Farmer	
NEILSON, James	3	A Child	
RODGERS, Catherine	30	Spinster	
BROWN, William	20	Labourer	
McCANN, James	25	Labourer	
HENDERSON, David	20	Labourer	
DOUGHERTY, Cornelius	20	Labourer	
McDONOGH, Thomas	50	Farmer	
McDONOGH, Catherine	50	Spinster	
McDONOGH, Catherine	50	Spinster	
McDONOGH, James	15	Farmer	
McDONOGH, Hugh	13	Farmer	
McDONOGH, Richard	11	Farmer	
McDONOGH, Thomas	2	A Child	
DONNELLY, Hugh	32	Labourer	
DONNELLY, Mary	28	Spinster	
KENNAN, Hugh	51	Labourer	
DONNELLY, Catherine	4	A Child	
KENNAN, Hugh	3	A Child	
KENNAN, Thomas	3	A Child	
BEATTY, John	28	Farmer	
BEATTY, Isabella	22	Spinster	
BEATTY, Stephen	2	A Child	
TRACY, James	30	Farmer	
TRACY, Rose	32	Spinster	
TRACY, Nancy	5	A Child	
TRACY, Margaret	2	A Child	
McCARRON, James	29	Farmer	
McCARRON, Jane	29	Spinster	
McCARRON, John	5	Labourer	
McCARRON, Fanny	3	A Child	
McQUAID, John	20	Labourer	
LEONARD, Robert	22	Labourer	
LEONARD, Jane	20	Spinster	
KELLY, John	24	Labourer	
BRUCE, Eliza	26	Spinster	
HARPER, Robert	30	Farmer	
HARPER, Jane	24	Spinster	
HARPER, Charles	35	Farmer	
FORSTER, John	24	Labourer	
LITTLE, Jane	21	Spinster	
HARPER, James	7	Labourer	
O'DONNELL, Anthony	19	Labourer	
BROWN, Manus	19	Labourer	
BROWN, Edward	20	Labourer	
COLLINS, Patrick	22	Labourer	
GALLAUGHER, John	26	Labourer	
DOUGHERTY, Charles	23	Labourer	
BEATTY, Rebecca	21	Spinster	
MULDOON, James	24	Labourer	

| SHIP: | CORNELIA | TO: | New York |
| SAIL DATE: | 19 April 1803 | FROM: | Londonderry |

NAME	AGE	OCCUPATION	RESIDENCE
KING, James	25	Farmer	
LENOX, John	30	Farmer	
COLHOUNE, William	30	Labourer	
CALDWELL, Patrick	25	Labourer	
CALDWELL, Jane	20	Spinster	
McIVER, Mary	17	Spinster	
McIVER, Judith	19	Spinster	
McIVER, Shane	25	Farmer	

| SHIP: | AMERICAN | | TO: | New York |

SHIP: AMERICAN   TO: New York

SAIL DATE: 19 April 1803   FROM: Londonderry

NAME	AGE	OCCUPATION	RESIDENCE
KERR, David	28	Farmer	Donegal
KERR, Hannah	25	Spinster	Donegal
VIRTUE, Robert	22	Farmer	Donegal
VIRTUE, Ann	25	Spinster	Donegal
THOMPSON, Alexander	21	Farmer	Fermanagh
JENKIN, L		Labourer	Fermanagh
BRANDEN, Andrew		Labourer	Fermanagh
MILLER, L		Labourer	Fermanagh
McCAFFERTY, James		Labourer	Fermanagh
WARD, John		Labourer	Fermanagh
FITZPATRICK, Robert		Labourer	Fermanagh
STINSON, Robert		Labourer	Fermanagh
TAYLOR, William		Labourer	Sligo
TAYLOR, Elinor		Spinster	Sligo
TAYLOR, Mary		Spinster	Sligo
LOUGHEAD, John		Labourer	Donegal
LOUGHEAD, R		Spinster	Donegal
LOUGHEAD, Robert		Labourer	Donegal
LOUGHEAD, John		Labourer	Donegal
WHITESIDE, John		Labourer	Donegal
WHITESIDE, Ann		Spinster	Donegal
JOHNSTON, Arthur		Farmer	Donegal
JOHNSTON, Mary		Spinster	Donegal
LOUGHEAD, Thomas	28	Labourer	Donegal
McCREA, James	20	Labourer	Ballintra
McCREA, John	25	Labourer	Ballintra
SPENCE, Barbara	24	Spinster	Ballintra
SPENCE, Catherine	23	Spinster	Ballintra
COULTER, John	23	Labourer	Petigo
CARR, Dennis	22	Labourer	Petigo
CARR, Catherine	21	Spinster	Petigo
TREMBLE, James	26	Farmer	Donegal
McGERAGH, Patrick	22	Farmer	Donegal
McKEE, Alexander	27	Farmer	Donegal
McKEE, Fanny	26	Spinster	Donegal
McMULLEN, Patrick	29	Labourer	Donegal
DEVARNEY, Hugh	26	Labourer	Monaghan
DEVINE, Bryan	28	Labourer	Monaghan
DEVINE, Ann	25	Spinster	Monaghan
McGINN, Mary	22	Spinster	Cavan
McGINN, Thomas	27	Labourer	Cavan
MURPHY, James	27	Labourer	Cavan
MURPHY, Thomas	23	Labourer	Cavan
McSWIGAN, Thomas	26	Labourer	Cavan
McSWIGAN, Mary	23	Spinster	Cavan
O'NEILL, Mark	25	Labourer	Drumquin
O'NEILL, Jane	23	Spinster	Drumquin
O'NEILL, Henry	17	Labourer	Drumquin

SHIP:	MOHAWK		TO: Philadelphia
SAIL DATE:	26 April 1803		FROM: Londonderry

NAME	AGE	OCCUPATION	RESIDENCE
CALLAGHAN, Neal	19	Labourer	Ardmalin
DOUGHERTY, Darby	25	Labourer	Ardmalin
THOMPSON, John	35	Labourer	Ardmalin
HETHRINGTON, Charles	40	Labourer	Dungannon
HETHRINGTON, Christy	36	Labourer	Dungannon
HETHRINGTON, Susanna	40		Dungannon
HETHRINGTON, Joseph	14		Dungannon
HETHRINGTON, Eliza	16		Dungannon
HETHRINGTON, George	10		Dungannon
WALKER, James	32	House Servant	Enniskillen
WALKER, Anne	30		Enniskillen
WALKER, Ralph	36	Labourer	Enniskillen
WALKER, Anne	32		Enniskillen
WOOD, Alexander	26	Labourer	Lisnaska
WOOD, Mary	20		Lisnaska
ALEXANDER, William	32	Labourer	Donagheady
ALEXANDER, Jane	30		Donagheady
ALEXANDER, James	11		Donagheady
ALEXANDER, Martha	10		Donagheady
BACON, William	28	Labourer	Taughbone
BACON, Elizabeth	27		Taughbone
BACON, William	12		Taughbone
McGRENAN, John	18	House Servant	Taughbone
McCAFFERTY, Pat	19	Labourer	Taughbone
DORAN, Thomas	23	Labourer	Taughbone
MARTIN, Anne	20		Enniskillen
DRUM, Thomas	36	Labourer	Enniskillen
DRUM, Nathaniel	34	Labourer	Enniskillen
SMYTH, Frances	29		Enniskillen
DRUM, William	20	Labourer	Enniskillen
DRUM, Mary	16		Enniskillen
LUNNY, Pat	20		Enniskillen
BATES, John	21	Labourer	Donamanagh
MURRAY, James	20	Labourer	Donamanagh
JONES, Richard	24	House Servant	Strabane
McANA, Barry	24	Labourer	Strabane
GLIN, William	25	Labourer	Letterkenny
McDADE, Owen	28	Labourer	Carne
HOPKINS, Robert	21	Labourer	Bolea
GRAHAM, Robert	20	Labourer	Bolea
PHILIPS, Abraham	35	Labourer	Urney
McCREA, Robert	30	House Servant	Strabane
DIVEN, Pat	28	House Servant	Strabane
FORRESTER, Henry	24	Labourer	Clonis
TAGGART, Samuel	30	Labourer	Clonis
TAGGART, Margaret	28		Clonis
NEELY, Elizabeth	21		Newtown Stewart
McCOY, John	20	Labourer	Clougher
HASTINGS, John	21	Labourer	Stewartstown
SIMPSON, John	25	Labourer	Stewartstown
WALKER, George	20	Labourer	Stewartstown
THOMPSON, Samuel	28	Labourer	Dungannon
THOMPSON, Anna	30		Dungannon
THOMPSON, Andrew	25	Labourer	Dungannon
THOMPSON, James	6		Dungannon
THOMPSON, Sarah	22		Dungannon
CAMPBELL, James	28	Labourer	Dungannon
CAMPBELL, Mary	20		Dungannon
BRADLEY, Patrick	19	House Servant	Londonderry
BRADLEY, Alexander	28	Labourer	Newtownstewart
ANDERSON, Archibald	19	Labourer	Armagh
TAIT, James	36	Labourer	Armagh

| SHIP: | MOHAWK | | TO: | Philadelphia |
| SAIL DATE: | 26 April 1803 | | FROM: | Londonderry |

NAME	AGE	OCCUPATION	RESIDENCE
McGONEGALL, James	25	Labourer	Buncrana
McAWARD, Terrol	21	Labourer	Buncrana
O'DONNELL, Patrick	20	Labourer	Buncrana
LYNCHAHIN, Denis	20	Labourer	Buncrana
DOUGHERTY, Neal	21	Labourer	Buncrana
KELLY, William	23	Labourer	Buncrana
CARTON, John	35	Labourer	Claggen
McCONAGHY, David	20	Labourer	Ballyarton
McQUISTIN, Robert	26	Labourer	Dungiven

SHIP:	ARDENT		TO: Baltimore
SAIL DATE: 26 April 1803			FROM: Londonderry

NAME	AGE	OCCUPATION	RESIDENCE
RAMSEY, Thomas	28	Farmer	Near Muff, Co Donegal
ELLIOTT, Hugh	60	Farmer	Rancel, Co Donegal
ELLIOTT, Mrs	54		Rancel, Co Donegal
ELLIOTT, James	20	Farmer	Rancel, Co Donegal
ELLIOTT, Hugh	14		Rancel, Co Donegal
ELLIOTT, Jean	18		Rancel, Co Donegal
RICHEY, James	58	Farmer	Doran, Co Donegal
RICHEY, Mrs	52		Doran, Co Donegal
RICHEY, William	18	Farmer	Doran, Co Donegal
RICHEY, Catherine	16		Doran, Co Donegal
RICHEY, Ann	14		Doran, Co Donegal
RICHEY, John	20	Farmer	Doran, Co Donegal
RICHEY, Andrew	12		Doran, Co Donegal
RICHEY, Ellen	10		Doran, Co Donegal
McKEE, Andrew	38	Farmer	Doran, Co Donegal
McKEE, Mrs	34		Doran, Co Donegal
RICHEY, Eliza	9		Doran, Co Donegal
McKEE, Nancy	16		Doran, Co Donegal
McKEE, Pat	14		Doran, Co Donegal
FINLAY, Eliza	57		Doran, Co Donegal
FINLAY, John	22	Farmer	Doran, Co Donegal
FINLAY, James	17	Farmer	Doran, Co Donegal
CUNIGAN, Pat	60	Drover	Killaughter, Co Donegal
MANILUS, James	26	Drover	Kilcar, Co Donegal
CLARK, Hugh	30	Farmer	Doran, Co Donegal
CLARK, Mrs (Sen)	28		Doran, Co Donegal
CLARK, James	17	Farmer	Doran, Co Donegal
CLARK, William	26	Farmer	Doran, Co Donegal
CLARK, Mrs (Jun)	22		Doran, Co Donegal
CLARK, Alexander	8		Doran, Co Donegal
RICHEY, Mrs	38		Doran, Co Donegal
RICHEY, George	9		Doran, Co Donegal
RICHEY, Charles	44	Farmer	Doran, Co Donegal
McCULLOGH, Andrew	40	Farmer	Doran, Co Donegal
McCULLOGH, Mrs	34		Doran, Co Donegal
McCULLOGH, Andrew	16		Doran, Co Donegal
McCULLOGH, Jean	14		Doran, Co Donegal
McCULLOGH, George	12		Doran, Co Donegal
McCULLOGH, Alexander	10		Doran, Co Donegal
MONTGOMERY, John	24	Gentleman	Killybegs, Co Donegal
JONES, John	20	Gentleman	Killybegs, Co Donegal
GRAHAM, William	22	Farmer	Tyrough, Co Donegal
GRAHAM, Francis	22	Farmer	Tyrough, Co Donegal
CUNNINGHAM, James	17		Gleneny, Co Donegal
CRAWFORD, John	28	Farmer	Ballybofey, Co Donegal
ERWIN, John	56	Farmer	Ballybofey, Co Donegal
CRAWFORD, George	32	Farmer	Doran, Co Donegal
BOGLE, Ann	14		Mt Charles, Co Donegal
GRAHAM, David	48	Farmer	Dergbridge, Co Tyrone
GRAHAM, Sarah	41		Dergbridge, Co Tyrone

SHIP:	JEFFERSON		TO: New York

SAIL DATE: 26 April 1803   FROM: Sligo

NAME	AGE	OCCUPATION	RESIDENCE
GONAGLE, Peter	40	Labourer	Sligo, Co Sligo
CHENTEN, James	26	Labourer	Cluntagh, Co Sligo
LEYONARD, Edmond	20	Labourer	Cluntagh, Co Sligo
WATERSON, Pat	55	Labourer	Cluntagh, Co Sligo
McGAN, John	32	Labourer	Carns, Co Sligo
WYMBS, Thomas	36	Dealer	Carns, Co Sligo
WYMBS, Michael	30	Dealer	Carns, Co Sligo
HAREGDON, Pat	41	Labourer	Moneygold, Co Sligo
HARKEN, John	26	Labourer	Grange, Co Sligo
KELLY, Francis	29	Labourer	Bunduff, Co Sligo
NELIS, James	27	Labourer	Creeny, Co Sligo
GILFEADER, Edmond	23	Labourer	Mt Temple, Co Sligo
REILY, Thomas	29	Labourer	Mt Temple, Co Sligo
McKEY, James	36	Labourer	Sligo, Co Sligo
CURRY, James	28	Labourer	Sligo, Co Sligo
GILMARTIN, Daniel	29	Labourer	Sligo, Co Sligo
FARRELL, Thomas	23	Labourer	Cluntagh, Co Sligo
HIGGINS, John	37	Labourer	Cluntagh, Co Sligo
KALENG, William	42	Labourer	Cluntagh, Co Sligo

SHIP:	SERPENT	TO:	Baltimore
SAIL DATE:	3 May 1803	FROM:	Londonderry

NAME	AGE	OCCUPATION	RESIDENCE
NEILSON, Joseph	26	Farmer	Strabane
NEILSON, Margaret	24		Strabane
NEILSON, Jane	14	Spinster	Strabane
NEILSON, Elizabeth	12	Spinster	Strabane
NEILSON, John	10		Strabane
NEILSON, James	7		Strabane
McCARTHY, Samuel	25	Labourer	Omagh
FALLS, David	25	Labourer	Omagh
TURNER, Samuel	30	Labourer	Strabane
NEILSON, John	27	Labourer	Strabane
MONNIGLE, Patrick	28	Labourer	Rossquill
McPEAK, Neal	30	Labourer	Rossquill
McCANN, Michael	40	Farmer	Rossquill
McCANN, Phelix	35	Farmer	Rossquill
McCANN, Patrick	28	Farmer	Rossquill
McCANN, Peter	18	Farmer	Rossquill
McCANN, Nelly	37		Rossquill
McCANN, Susan	40		Rossquill
McCANN, Hannah	16	Spinster	Rossquill
McCANN, Mary	14	Spinster	Rossquill
McBRIDE, James	25	Farmer	Rossquill
McBRIDE, Catherine	24		Rossquill
CORBITT, Peter	25	Farmer	Rathmullen
CORBITT, Isabella	23		Rathmullen
MUNDELL, John	40	Farmer	Gortgarn
MUNDELL, Margaret	39		Gortgarn
MUNDELL, Samuel	46	Farmer	Gortgarn
MUNDELL, William John	25	Farmer	Gortgarn
MUNDELL, Isabella	37		Gortgarn
MUNDELL, Isabella	20	Spinster	Gortgarn
MUNDELL, Jane	16	Spinster	Gortgarn
MUNDELL, Mary	14	Spinster	Gortgarn
MUNDELL, Elizabeth	12	Spinster	Gortgarn
CRAIG, Margaret	36		Gortgarn
BAIRD, George	25	Farmer	Gortgarn
BAIRD, Samuel,	22	Farmer	Gortgarn
BAIRD, Mary	24		Gortgarn
BAIRD, Rahcel	25	Spinster	Gortgarn
KENEDY, Peter	27	Farmer	Gortgarn
KENEDY, Margaret	25		Gortgarn
KENEDY, Emelia	6		Gortgarn
REED, James	40	Farmer	Maghera
REED, Agnes	37		Maghera
REED, Sally	15	Spinster	Maghera
McCOOL, Mary	45		Maghera
McCOOL, James	24	Farmer	Maghera
McCOOL, John	20	Farmer	Maghera
ROSS, Nelly	35		Maghera
ROSS, James	18	Labourer	Maghera

SHIP:	STRAFFORD		TO:	Philadelphia
SAIL DATE:	14 May 1803		FROM:	Londonderry

NAME	AGE	OCCUPATION	RESIDENCE
McGAN, John	34	Farmer	Coagh
McGAN, Elizabeth	30	Spinster	Coagh
McGAN, Sarah	2		Coagh
McGAN, Elinor		Infant	Coagh
WALKER, William	30	Farmer	Coagh
WALKER, John	9	Farmer	Coagh
WALKER, Mary Anne	20	Spinster	Coagh
WALKER, Elizabeth	18	Spinster	Coagh
MITCHELL, William	20	Farmer	Cumber
CONIGHAM, Thomas	18	Farmer	Ballymoney
STEWART, Alexander	20	Labourer	Kelraghts
MOORE, John	19	Labourer	Loughgin
HAMILTON, James	23	Labourer	Loughgin
SMILY, William	23	Labourer	Kelraghts
CLARKE, Edward	40	Farmer	Enniskillen
MILLEY, John	45	Farmer	Enniskillen
LOUGHRIDGE, William	30	Farmer	Cookstown
LOUGHRIDGE, Margaret	24		Cookstown
LOUGHRIDGE, Jane	7		Cookstown
LOUGHRIDGE, James	5		Cookstown
LOUGHRIDGE, Eliza	2		Cookstown
HARKIN, Nancy	30	Seamstress	Birdstown
HARKIN, Nelly	4		Birdstown
HARKIN, William	6		Birdstown
CHAMBERS, John	20	Farmer	County Tyrone
GRAY, WIlliam	24	Farmer	County Tyrone
RALSTON, James	45	Farmer	County Tyrone
RALSTON, Mary	40		County Tyrone
RALSTON,James	15		County Tyrone
RALSTON, Mary	12		County Tyrone
RALSTON, David	9		County Tyrone
RALSTON, Joseph	5		County Tyrone
RALSTON, Anne	2		County Tyrone
RALSTON, Anne	44	Seamstress	County Tyrone
RALSTON, Robert	19	Labourer	County Tyrone
RALSTON, David	15	Labourer	County Tyrone
RALSTON, John	11		County Tyrone
RALSTON, Jane	8		County Tyrone
RALSTON, Anne	5		County Tyrone
RALSTON, Joseph	2		County Tyrone
RALSTON, John	40	Farmer	County Tyrone
RALSTON, Sarah	40	Seamstress	County Tyrone
RALSTON, David	9		County Tyrone
RALSTON, Andrew	7		County Tyrone
RALSTON, William	3		County Tyrone
RALSTON, James	5		County Tyrone
SHEAN, Elinor	60		County Down
ANDERSON, Mary	24		County Down
ANDERSON, Mary	2		County Down
WILSON, John	22	Farmer	
CARR, William	20	Farmer	
MOORE, James	19	Farmer	Ballykelly

SHIP:	PATTY		TO:	Philadelphia
SAIL DATE:	14 May 1803		FROM:	Warrenpoint

NAME	AGE	OCCUPATION	RESIDENCE
GRIFFIS, William	34	Labourer	Co Down
HURS, Andrew	30	Labourer	Co Down
KENEDY, John	41	Labourer	Co Down
McBRIDE, Samuel	28	Labourer	Co Tyrone
GIBSON, John	50	Farmer	Co Tyrone
LYNCH, Patrick	27	Labourer	Co Tyrone
HUNTER, David	24	Labourer	Co Tyrone
HUNTER, Ann	22	Spinster	Co Tyrone
HUNTER, David	28	Labourer	Co Tyrone
HUNTER, Edward	34	Labourer	Co Tyrone
HUNTER, George	14	Labourer	Co Tyrone
ARMSTRONG, Alexander	29	Labourer	Co Armagh
HARVEY, Mary	45	Spinster	Co Armagh
HARVEY, Eliza	23	Spinster	Co Armagh
HARVEY, Robert	48	Farmer	Co Armagh
BROWN, Biddy	38	Spinster	Co Down
WILLIAMS, Henry	28	Gentleman	Co Armagh
PATTON, Samuel	32	Labourer	Co Down
PATTON, Joseph	36	Labourer	Co Down
TILFORDE, George	28	Labourer	Co Down
BLAIR, John	29	Labourer	Co Down
McDALE, John	36	Labourer	Co Down
POTTS, Walter	25	Labourer	Co Down
RONEY, William	19	Labourer	Co Down
EAKIN, James	46	Farmer	Co Down
EAKIN, Samuel	50	Farmer	Co Down
FITZPATRICK, James	37	Farmer	Co Down
FITZPATRICK, Mary	32	Spinster	Co Down
MAUGHER, Edward	26	Labourer	Queens County
FLEMING, John	24	Labourer	Queens County
DICK, Thomas	32	Farmer	Co Down
NELSON, James	28	Farmer	Co Down
ARMSTRONG, John	29	Farmer	Co Down

SHIP:	ACTIVE		TO:	Philadelphia
SAIL DATE:	14 May 1803		FROM:	Newry

NAME	AGE	OCCUPATION	RESIDENCE
MOORE, James	21	Clerk	
RENDLES, James	40	Labourer	
RENDLES, John	38	Labourer	
RENDLES, Eliza	16		
RENDLES, Thomas	12	Labourer	
BARNETT, John	38	Labourer	
BARNETT, Margaret	34		
LAVERTY, Eliza	20		
BARNETT, Andrew	24	Labourer	
BARNETT, Annabella	20		
BARNETT, Martha	18		
MILLS, Robert	40	Labourer	
MILLS, Frances	28	Labourer	
BARNETT, Eliza	16		
BARNET, Jane	12		
STEWART, William	50	Labourer	
STEWART, Margret	38		
STEWART, Ann	24		
STEWART, Agness	20		

NAME	AGE	OCCUPATION	RESIDENCE
ALLEN, Isabella	32		Market-Hill
COLLINS, John	36	Labourer	Market-Hill
CRAWLEY, Patrick	39	Labourer	Market-Hill
CRAWLEY, Mary	39		Market-Hill
BURDEN, Richard	28	Labourer	Fentona
FARREL, James	40	Labourer	Stewartstown
PHILIPS, Patrick	24	Labourer	Strabane
ROONEY, Thomas	40	Labourer	Banbridge
MARTIN, Mary	20		Banbridge
BROTHERS, Charlotte	26		Banbridge
COLLINS, Isaac	30	Labourer	Monaghan
MARTIN, John	36	Labourer	Monaghan
BROTHERS, John	30	Labourer	Monaghan
LEWIS, Thomas	30	Labourer	Monaghan
MICHAEL, John	30	Labourer	Dundalk
SLEITH, William	23	Labourer	Dundalk
ELLS, Henry	30	Labourer	Newry
TURE, Thomas	39	Labourer	Newry
SMITH, Thomas	37	Labourer	Rathfriland
BROTHERS, Rebecca	45		Newry
PHILIPS, Benjamin	30	Labourer	Dundalk
MYHOOD, Hanna	25		Newry
DOWNS, James	30	Labourer	Cootehill
CRAWLY, Samuel	35	Labourer	Cootehill
BURDEN, John	32	Labourer	Ballybery
BARDER, Sarah	31		Ballybery
DEBLOIS, Rebecca	24		Ballyconnell
WITHORN, Eliza	23		Killyshandon
CAHOONE, Mary	22		Cavan
OVERING, Mary	25		Cavan

SHIP:	HOPEWELL		TO:	New York
SAIL DATE:	7 June 1803		FROM:	Newry

NAME	AGE	OCCUPATION	RESIDENCE
DOWNEY, Peter	22	Labourer	
THORNBURY, William	40	Labourer	
DALEY, William	30	Labourer	
TERRIGAN, George	32	Labourer	
MARTIN, William	36	Labourer	
SMYLEY, Samuel	35	Labourer	
McLEAVERETT, John	30	Labourer	
CULLAGER, Pat	20	Labourer	
HUMPHRIES, David	52	Labourer	
HUMPHRIES, Joseph	26	Labourer	
HUMPHRIES, Robert	40	Labourer	
HUMPHRIES, Moses	17	Labourer	
COUSER, James	18	Labourer	
HUMPHRIES, Robert	19	Labourer	
REED, James	20	Labourer	
McLEHERRY, Thomas	21	Labourer	
ANDERSON, John	25	Labourer	

SHIP:	WILMINGTON			TO:	New York
SAIL DATE:	12 July 1803			FROM:	Belfast

NAME	AGE	OCCUPATION	RESIDENCE
HOUSTON, John	30	Farmer	
HOUSTON, Mrs	27		
HOUSTON, ?	7		
HOUSTON, ?	5		
HOUSTON, ?	2		
STEWART, Robert	27	Farmer	
STEWART, Mrs	24		
STEWART, ?	2	Child	
GALWAY, James	18	Farmer	
ALLEN, Thomas	25	Farmer	
ERSKIN, William	32	Farmer	
DICK, Isabella	16		
CROSS, John	35	Farmer	
CROZIER, William	26	Farmer	
McHENRY, Henry	40	Gentleman	
READ, Henry	30	Gentleman	
CURRY, Jane	36		
CURRY, Mary	14		
CURRY, Eliza	12		
CURRY, John	9		
WARNICK, Robert	30	Gentleman	
GARRETT, Henry	33	Farmer	
GARRETT, S Ann	27		
MANCALLY, Mary	23		
BROWNE, John	45	Gentleman	
JACKSON, Robert	30	Gentleman	
MURPHY, John	28	Gentleman	
THOMPSON, John	26	Gentleman	
McCRELLOS, Thomas	34	Farmer	
McCONAGHY, Thomas	27	Farmer	
CAMERON, John	39	Farmer	
CAMERON, Lavinia	20		
CAMERON, Agnus	17		
CAMERON, Martha	14		
CAMERON, Elinor	9		
CHESTNUT, Samuel	30	Gentleman	
CAMERON, Mary	36		

SHIP:	MARGARET	TO: Wiscasset, USA
SAIL DATE:	12 July 1803	FROM: Dublin

NAME	AGE	OCCUPATION	RESIDENCE
IRWIN, Edward	50	Labourer	Wexford
PHILLIPS, George	30	Labourer	Wexford
MAGUIRE, Thomas	32	Labourer	Wexford
IRWIN, Patrick	31	Labourer	Wexford
CAVANAGH, James	34	Labourer	Wexford
BEST, Thomas	22	Labourer	Wexford
IRWIN, Mary	40		Wexford
IRWIN, Ann	9		Wexford

SHIP:	SALLY		TO:	New York
SAIL DATE: 6 August 1803			FROM:	Dublin

NAME	AGE	OCCUPATION	RESIDENCE
FLOOD, Elizabeth	24	Spinster	Dublin
FLOOD, Alice	22	Spinster	Dublin
KELLY, Margaret	45	Spinster	Dublin
PURFIELD, Alicia	18	Spinster	Dublin
EAGLE, Ann	10	Child	Dublin
EAGLE, George	9	Child	Dublin
BENNETT, Mary	30	Spinster	Dublin
CAMPBELL, Michael	24	Labourer	Dublin
FALLIS, Nancy	20	Spinster	Dublin
GRAND, James	17	Labourer	Scotch
KELLY, Hugh	24	Labourer	Dublin
FITZPATRICK, Bernard	38	Farmer	Tullamore
FITZPATRICK, Ellen	28		Tullamore
FITZPATRICK, Mary		Child (Infant)	Tullamore
LYONS, John	30		Tullamore

| SHIP: | GEORGE | TO: New York |
| SAIL DATE: 20 August 1803 | | FROM: Dublin |

NAME	AGE	OCCUPATION	RESIDENCE
O'BRIEN, John	28	Clerk	Dublin
BANNON, Michael	23	Farmer	Mayo
LYONS, John	30	Farmer	Tullamore
EVANS, Mark	30	Farmer	Queens County
EVANS, Mary (his wife)			Queens County
HENNERY, James	25	Farmer	Dublin County
DOYLE, Patrick	20	Farmer	Mayo
FITZPATRICK, Bernard	36	Farmer	Tullamore
His wife			Tullamore
His child			Tullamore
O'HARA, Henry	23	Farmer	Clare

SHIP:	EAGLE		TO: New York
SAIL DATE: 30 August 1803			FROM: Belfast

NAME	AGE	OCCUPATION	RESIDIENCE
SMALL, Robert	27	Labourer	Ballymoney
CONORY, William	40	Farmer	State of Pensylvania
McKEOWN, Alexander	18	Labourer	Belfast
WILLIAMSON, William	25	Labourer	Kilinchy
MISKELLY, Owen	25	Labourer	Kilinchy
MISKELLY, Kitty		Spinster	Kilinchy
MAGIL, William	23	Labourer	Kilinchy
WELSH, Roger	24	Labourer	Kilinchy
REID, James	22	Labourer	Saintfield
ARMSTRONG, Thomas	31	Farmer	Clonfeakle
ARMSTRONG, Mary		Spinster	Clonfeakle
TREANOR, John	22	Farmer	Kilinchy
MURPHY, John	24	Labourer	Kilinchy
ORR, Alexander	21	Gentleman	Ballymoney
BOYD, James	30	Merchant	Near Ballymena
WILEY, Samuel B	30	Clergyman	Philadelphia
MOORHEAD, John	24	Merchant	Antrim
HEYLAND, Marcus	22	Merchant	Coleraine
FREELAND, William	20	Farmer	Co Armagh
DEYRINAN, William	25	Labourer	Drumbo
MILD, James	25	Farmer	Aughaloo
CALDWELL, James	22	Merchant	Ballymoney
ORR, Mrs	40	Spinster	Portglenone
HOUSTON, Mrs		Spinster	Tobermore
BREENE, John	15	Farmer	Killinchy
McNEILL, Samuel	20	Grocer	Ballymena
CAMPBELL, James	30	Labourer	Carmoney
MINISS, Samuel	21	Labourer	Saintfield
McAULEY, James	22	Labourer	Saintfield
DIXON, William	22	Labourer	Saintfield
MOORE, Samuel	18	Gentleman	Portglenone
GRAHAM, Alexander	34	MD	Last Residence Glasgow
NEILSON, Thomas	24	Merchant	Ballinderry
NEILSON, Samuel	18	None	Ballinderry
NEILSON, Robert	21	Merchant	Ballinderry
GARRET, James	28	Merchant	Annahilt

SHIP:	GEORGE		TO: New York
SAIL DATE: 30 August 1803			FROM: Dublin

NAME	AGE	OCCUPATION	RESIDENCE
O'BRIEN, John	28	Clerk	Dublin
BANNON, Michael	23	Farmer	Mayo
LYONS, John	30	Farmer	Tullamore
EVANS, Mark	30	Farmer	Queens County
EVANS, Ann (his wife)			Queens County
HENNESY, James	25	Labourer	Dublin
DOYLE, Patrick	20	Farmer	Mayo
FITZPATRICK, Bernard	36	Farmer	Tullamore
His wife			Tullamore
His child			Tullamore
O'HARA, Henry	23	Farmer	Clare
ROE, Peter	30	Merchant	Ross
FRENCH, Shepherd	45	Merchant	Carrick-on-Suir
JOYCE, Mathew	18	Clerk	Dublin
MADDEN, Hugh	30	Clerk	Dublin

SHIP:	SUSAN		TO:	New York
SAIL DATE:	6 September 1803		FROM:	Dublin

NAME	AGE	OCCUPATION	RESIDENCE
O'CONNOR, John		Master	)
WYLY, Thomas		First Mate	)
ROACHE, Patrick		Second Mate	)
HOWARD, Thomas		Mariner	)
BROWNE, Thomas		Mariner	)
ANDERSON, George		Mariner	)
SCULLY, Timothy		Mariner	)
DOYLE, Daniel		Mariner	) Citizens of the
GREW, Daniel		Mariner	) United States of
DOOLITTLE, George		Apprentice	) North America
BOOBY, Valentine		Apprentice	)
PETERS, John		Cook	)
HANDSAW, Isaac		Cook	)
BELL, Abraham	28	Merchant	New York
BLEAKLY, Robert	26	Linen Merchant	Armagh
BLEAKLY, David	24	Linen Merchant	Armagh
MATHEWS, Mrs	45		L'Derry
GALLAGHER, Simon Felix	45	Catholic Pastor	Charleston
CARBERY, John	36	Merchant	Danish Island
WATTERS, John	27	Clerk	Navan
CURTIS, John	28	Super Cargo	Dublin
HORNRIDGE, James	25	Surgeon	New York
ROBERTS, Thomas	25	Farmer	England
NORTH, John	36	Gentleman	America
TOOLE, Laurence	22	Labourer	Dublin
FLEMING, Walter	21	Clerk	New York
MADDIN, Hugh	23	Clerk	Dublin
MORRIS, Roger	28	Clerk	Dublin
SEDGEWICK, William	36	Clerk	Dublin
FULHAM, Arthur	12		Edinderry
HUGHES, Jane	22		Co Down
KELLY, Mary	40		Dublin
MATHEWS, Mary	12		Dublin
O'BRIEN, Mary	9		Dublin
O'BRIEN, Anne	8		Dublin
LANGLEY, Eliza	22		Kilkenny
NOROLAN, Margaret	22		Kilkenny
O'CONNOR, Biddy	14		Wexford
LARKIN, Mary	16		Wexford
REILLY, Mary Ann	22		Dublin

SHIP:	FORTITUDE		TO: New York
SAIL DATE: 6 September 1803			FROM: Cork

NAME	AGE	OCCUPATION	RESIDENCDE
SCULLY, John Sullivan	35	Merchant	Cork
SULLIVAN, Mary	28	His wife	Cork
RYAN, James	34	Farmer	Bantry
RYAN, Mary	30	Wife to above	Bantry
LONG, James	22	Shopkeeper	Bantry
SULLIVAN, Denis	21	Shopkeeper	Bantry
SULLIVAN, Cornelius	17	Farmer	Bantry
BARRY, John	25	Farmer	Bantry
HARTE, Mary	40	Sailor's wife	Cove
HARTE, Mary	10	Child to Sailor's Wife	Cove
HARTE, John	5	Child to Sailor's wife	Cove
JOHNSON, Thomas	30	Clerk	Cork
STEWART, Mary	55	Gentlewoman	Cork
DEVAYNE, William	60	Gentleman	Exeter, Devon - now in Cork
DEVAYNE, Harriott	24	Daughter to above	Exeter, Devon - now in Cork
DEVAYNE, Charlotte	22	Daughter to above	Exeter, Devon - now in Cork
HUGHES, James	30	Gentleman	Richmond, America - now in Cork
HUGHES, Mary	28	Wife to above	Richmond, America - now in Cork

SHIP:	AMERICAN		TO:	New York
SAIL DATE:	13 September 1803		FROM:	Londonderry

NAME	AGE	OCCUPATION	RESIDENCE
THOMPSON, Alexander	28	Master	New York
VERNON, John	25	1st Mate	New York
SUTHERLAND, David	32	2nd Mate	New York
WOOD, James	28	Seaman	New York
CORNALE, Joseph J	22	Seaman	New York
MARTIN, Richard	20	Seaman	New York
FINEGAN, Bakey	30	Seaman	New York
DE OSTENU, Peter	22	Seaman	New York
EWING, John	36	Seaman	New York
JOHNSTON, John	30	Cook	New York
NESBITT, Robert	18	Seaman	New York
ATRIDGE, George	16	Seaman	New York
PATTON, John	34	Merchant	New York
BORELAND, Robert	20	Farmer	Strabane
BORELAND, Mary	19	Spinster	Strabane
McGHEE, Hannah	45	Spinster	Strabane
McGOWAN, Edward	25	Labourer	Tamlaght, Co Derry
DUNN, William	25	Farmer	Gillygordon
BUCHANNAN, Thomas	22	Farmer	Gillygordon
DONAHY, John	21	Labourer	N T Lamavady
DOUGHERTY, James	23	Labourer	Ramullon
PATTERSON, John	30	Farmer	Moneymore
PATTERSON, Mathew	27	Farmer	Moneymore
PATTERSON, George	26	Farmer	Moneymore
PATTERSON, Eliza	20	Farmer	Moneymore
CORMICK, James	28	Clerk	Strabane
CORMICK, Rebecca	20	Spinster	Strabane
McKINLEY, Alexander	23	Farmer	Strabane
TORBET, John	18	Labourer	Co Tyrone
MILLER, Thomas	28	Farmer	Coagh
MILLER, David	24	Farmer	Coagh
MILLER, Martha	50	Farmer	Coagh
MILLER, Elizabeth	23	Spinster	Coagh
FOSTER, Robert	22	Farmer	Coagh
FOSTER, Martha	22	Spinster	Coagh
BROWNE, William	34	Farmer	Coagh
BROWN, Margaret	26	Spinster	Coagh
McGOWAN, Philip	34	Farmer	Gleek Tamlaght
McGOWAN, Grace	27	Spinster	Gleek Tamlaght
McGOWAN, Philip Jun	12		Gleek Tamlaght
McKENNEY, John	38	Merchant	New York
BIRKET, David	30	Farmer	Castlefin
BEATTY, William	25	Trader	New York
LINDSAY, George	32	Farmer	Pettigoe
COOK, William	26	Farmer	Pettigoe
COCKRAN, Isaac	27	Merchant	New York
McFARLAND, James	24	Farmer	Co Tyrone
McINTIRE, Alexander	29	Farmer	Waterside, L'Derry
McCLARY, Edward	21	Farmer	Tamlaght, Co Derry
McGHEE, Mary	38	Spinster	Cookstown

SHIP:	SUSAN		TO:	New York
SAIL DATE:	13 September 1803		FROM:	Dublin

NAME	AGE	OCCUPATION	RESIDENCE
PRICE, John	35	Surgeon	New York
DOWDAL, Thomas	25	Labourer	Dublin
GAVAN, John	30	Attorney	Dublin
FLOOD, Thomas	20	Clerk	Dublin
FLINN, Andrew	23	Clerk	Dublin
SERMOTT, Patrick	25	Farmer	Wexford
MURPHY, Francis	50	Farmer	America
MURPHY, Owen	25	Farmer	Co Monaghan
CONNOR, Andrew	45	Merchant	Dublin

SHIP:	SNOW GEORGE		TO:	Philadelphia
SAIL DATE:	27 September 1803		FROM:	Belfast

NAME	AGE	OCCUPATION	RESIDENCE
LEE, Ephraim	26	Farmer	Killishandow, Cavan
LEE, Edward	23	Farmer	Killishandow, Cavan
GABBY, Hugh	18	Labourer	Killinchy, Down
WALSH, Robert	22	Dealer	Downpatrick, Down
FULTON, Alexander	34	Farmer	Loughgill, Down
KELLY, Thomas	36	Farmer	Grange, Down
DONELLY, Edward	27	Farmer	Lessan, Tyrone
LOWRY, William	29	Labourer	Killinchy, Down
SERVICE, Thomas	18	Labourer	Brocham, Antrim
DAWSON, Sarah	17		Connor, Antrim
TOOLE, Marcus	39	Servant	Belfast, Antrim
TOOLE, Jane	28		Belfast, Antrim
DODDS, John	30	Farmer	Dromall, Antrim
WILSON, Henry	24	Schoolmaster	Belfast, Antrim
THOMPSON, John	28	Dealer	Ballymoney, Antrim
MULLAN, Patrick	21	Dealer	Tynan, Armagh
STRACHAN, James	20	Farmer	Connor, Antrim
JOHNSON, John	19	Farmer	Connor, Antrim
BYST, Nathaniel	30	Dealer	Glencany, Antrim
DEVELIN, Jane	32		Ballymon, Armagh
DEVELIN, Roger	35	Farmer	Ballymon, Armagh
McKEY, Patrick	38	Farmer	Drumgoland, Down
STEWART, Alexander	21	Farmer	Tullylisk, Down
GANET, James	30	Dealer	Annahilt, Down
TIMOLY, Mathew	28	Labourer	Ballymagaw, Down
ARMSTRONG, Thomas	31	Farmer	Clonfeecle, Armagh
ARMSTRONG, Mary	27		Clonfeecle, Armagh
MATHEWS, Thomas	27	Dealer	Belfast, Antrim
MATHEWS, Eliza	25		Belfast, Antrim
WILSON, Joseph	22	Dealer	Belfast, Antrim
PUMPHEY, John	29	Farmer	Belfast, Antrim

SHIP:	BETSY		TO: New York
SAIL DATE: 27 September 1803			FROM: Newry

NAME	AGE	OCCUPATION	RESIDENCE
KILBREATH, James	25	Farmer	Kilkeel
KILBREATH, Jane	26		Kilkeel
MURRAY, Pat	28	Labourer	Hillsborough
MURRAY, Sarah	26		Hillsborough
SMITH, Robert	28	Farmer	Clough
SMITH, Jenny	26		Clough
CONWEL, James	28	Farmer	Armagh
CONWEL, Catharine	27		Armagh
CONWEL, Anthony	26	Farmer	Armagh
CONWEL, Bernard	25	Farmer	Armagh
CONWEL, Jeremiah	24	Farmer	Armagh
BURNS, Michael	25	Labourer	Armagh
TEDFORD, George	28	Labourer	Down
TEDFORD, Eliza	28		Down
WESTON, Rachael	20	Lady	Charlestown, America
McCULLOUGH, Patt	26	Farmer	Armagh
McCULLOUGH, Sally	27	Farmer	Armagh
CASSIDY, Patt	17	Farmer	Armagh
HUMPHRY, John	32	Merchant	Richmond, America, at present Lisburn, Ireland
McLERANEY, Owen	22	Labourer	Carrickadrummond
MOORE, James	45	Labourer	Cranfield
SMALL, Nelly	30	Labourer	Down
PATTERSON, Samuel	21	Labourer	Grange

SHIP:	LADY WASHINGTON	TO:	Charleston
SAIL DATE:	27 September 1803	FROM:	Belfast

NAME	AGE	OCCUPATION	RESIDENCE
McCANCE, Jane	54		Blackmingo, South Carolina
CRAIG, William	54	Farmer	Magheradroll, Co Down
CRAIG, Agnes his wife			Magheradroll, Co Down
His child			Magheradroll, Co Down
His servant boy			Magheradroll, Co Down
McCANCE, Hugh	55	Farmer	Magheradroll, Co Down
McCANCE, Elizabeth	57		Magheradroll, Co Down
His wife			
McCANCE, Hugh his son	19		Magheradroll, Co Down
McCANCE, Samuel his son	22		Magheradroll, Co Down
McCANCE, Jane	19		Magheradroll, Co Down
BLACKWOOD, John	15	Farmer	Clough
BELL, David	26	Merchant	Belfast, Co Antrim
CARSON, Samuel	36	Merchant	Belfast, Co Antrim
O'NEILL, Arthur	24	Farmer	Drumarra, Co Down
LESLIE, Samuel	22	Farmer	Kilmore, Co Down
LESLIE, William	20	Farmer	Kilmore, Co Down
WILSON, John	43	Farmer	Ballycann, Co Down
His wife	35	Farmer	Ballycann, Co Down
HOEY, William	18	Farmer	Ballykill, Co Antrim
YOUNG, John	22	Labourer	Glenavy, Co Antrim
SHERLOCK, John	23	Labourer	Glenavy, Co Antrim
RABB, Samuel	23	Farmer	Ballynahinch, Co Antrim
CALDWELL, Thomas	20	Labourer	Broad Island
CALDWELL, William	18	Labourer	Broad Island
LAUMONT, Widow			Charleston, South Carolina
LOWRY, John	35	Farmer	Garvagh, Co Down

| SHIP: | INDEPENDENCE | | TO: | New York |
| SAIL DATE: | 8 November 1803 | | FROM: | Londonderry |

NAME	AGE	OCCUPATION	RESIDENCE
FLEMING, Mathias	27	Captain	New York
SMYTH, Joseph	28	Mate	New York
WILSON, Samuel	29	Seaman	New York
MILLER, Daniel	30	Cook	New York
BARRY, William	13	Boy	New York
JOHNSTON, Old	24	Seaman	New York
HARMAN, John	20	Seaman	New York
TOWERS, Frank	28	Seaman	New York
MASON, Benjamin F	30	Seaman	New York
McKELVY, Edward	35	Farmer	Letterkenny
McKELVY, Mrs	35	Housewife	Letterkenny
Three children to the			Letterkenny
above.			
CREYON, Luke	20	Labourer	Sligo
CREYON, Roger	18	Labourer	Sligo
STEWART, John C	24	Farmer	Sligo
WOOD, Francis	26	Labourer	Letterkenny
WOOD, Isabella with			Letterkenny
her infant child.			
LEARY, Thomas	28	Farmer	Raphoe
LEARY, Michael	20	Farmer	Raphoe
CAFFRY, Rose	18	Spinster	Raphoe
LAUGHLIN, Thomas	18	Farmer	Raphoe
CAFFRY, Thomas	20	Labourer	Raphoe
HOPKINS, John	24	Labourer	Letterkenny
FISHER, John	26	Labourer	Letterkenny
LATEMORE, William	30	Labourer	Letterkenny
LATEMORE, Mary	29	Labourer	Letterkenny
WARD, James	25	Labourer	Letterkenny
TORY, Henry	28	Labourer	Letterkenny
ROBINSON, Joseph	20	Labourer	Letterkenny
MILLER, Margaret	20	Spinster	Derry
McDALE, Mathew	36	Labourer	Carrickfergus
McDALE, J	20	Spinster	Carrickfergus

SHIP:	VENUS		TO: Norfolk, America
SAIL DATE: 14 November 1803			FROM: Dublin

NAME	AGE	OCCUPATION	RESIDENCE
SHERMAN, John	18	Merchant	Dublin, No 13 Little Britain Street
ROONEY, Edward	30	Merchant	Smithfield No 45
McENTIRE, George	23	Physician	No 17 Crampton Court
McENTIRE, Mrs	22		No 17 Crampton Court
DEMPSY, Edward	22	Farmer	Klinbullock, Kings County
DEMSEY, Thomas	18	Farmer	Klinbullock, Kings County
DEMSEY, Mary	50		Klinbullock, Kings County
DEMSEY, Ester	20		Klinbullock, Kings County
DEMSEY, Judy	19		Klinbullock, Kings County
DEMSEY, Catherine	16		Klinbullock, Kings County
BEST, Thomas	17	Gentleman	Smithfield

| SHIP: | FORTITUDE | | TO: New York |
| SAIL DATE: 21 February 1804 | | | FROM: Cork |

NAME	AGE	OCCUPATION	RESIDENCE
MAHONY, Margaret	30	Gentlewoman	Dunmanaway
MAHONY, Ann	9	daughter to above	Dunmanaway
BURKE, Goody	30	Gentlewoman	Kilkenny
BURKE, Ellen	12	daughter to above	Kilkenny
BURKE, Edward	9	brother to above	Kilkenny
BURKE, Biddy	7	sister to above	Kilkenny
BURKE, Denis	5	brother to above	Kilkenny
BRIEN, John	55	Farmer	County Waterford
CORBETT, Pierce	22	Farmer	County Waterford
GRACE, Samuel	19	Farmer	Co Cork
MACKAY, Thomas	30	Farmer	Co Cork
MACKAY, Ellen	25	wife to above	Co Cork
MACKAY, Ellen	2	daughter to above	Co Cork
BRYAN, Thomas	22	Farmer	Co Cork
BROOKS, Thomas	36	Gentleman	Co Cork
FLANIGAN, Denis	28	Farmer	Co Limerick
GRADY, Daniel	25	Farmer	Co Kerry
GRADY, Francis	23	Farmer	Co Kerry
GRADY, Tim	21	Farmer	Co Kerry
CASHMAN, Charles	16	Farmer	Co Cork
BOND, Ann	39	Gentlewoman	Cork
BOND, Mary	17	daughter to above	Cork
BOND, Ellen	9	daughter to above	Cork

SHIP:	GEORGE		TO: New York
SAIL DATE: 28 February 1804			FROM: Belfast

NAME	AGE	OCCUPATION	RESIDENCE
SMITH, Andrew	24	Farmer	Downe
SPROWL, James	30	Farmer	Downe
COCHRAN, Alexander	36	Farmer	Downe
COCHRAN, Agnes	28	Spinster and 4 children from 1 - 8 years old	Downe
MAULIN, Elenor	70	Spinster	Downe
FLEMING, Margaret	20	Spinster	Downe
HINGEN, William	20	Gentleman	Drumara
O'HAMILL, Peter	27	Labourer	Antrim
DUNCAN, Thomas	18	Labourer	Antrim
JOHNSTON, John	50	Farmer	Antrim
CROTHERS, John	44	Farmer	Antrim
CROTHERS, William	34	Farmer	Antrim
CROTHERS, Robert	36	Farmer	Antrim
CROTHERS, Lucy	30	Spinster and 4 children from 1 - 8 years old	Antrim
GRAY, Thomas	30	Farmer	Antrim
GRAY, Jane	27	Spinster	Antrim
WILLSON, Hans	24	Farmer	Bangor
TEMPLETON, Edward	20	Farmer	Coleraine
TEMPLETON, Jane	18	Spinster	Coleraine
DAWSON, John	18	Farmer	Antrim
REA, David	24	Farmer	Downe

SHIP:	PRUDENCE		TO: Philadelphia
SAIL DATE: 6 March 1804			FROM: Dublin

NAME	AGE	OCCUPATION	RESIDENCE
MAITLAND, Thomas	22	Farmer	Baltinglass, Co Wicklow
MAITLAND, Ann and	56		Baltinglass, Co Wicklow
child	7		Baltinglass, Co Wicklow
MAITLAND, Mary Ann	19		Baltinglass, Co Wicklow
BARRY, James	25	Apothecary	Dublin City
McDERMOTT, John	26	Clerk	Dublin City
McCARTY, James	26	Clerk	Dublin City
GITTEN, John	30	Clerk	Dublin City
and child	8		Dublin City
HINES, Jane	22		Glasnevin, Co Dublin
NIXON, John	26	Farmer	Manor Hamilton, Co Leitrim
IRWIN, John	27	Farmer	Manor Hamilton, Co Leitrim
GORE, James	24	Clerk	Dublin City

SHIP:	EAGLE		TO:	New York

SAIL DATE: 15 March 1804   FROM: Belfast

NAME	AGE	OCCUPATION	RESIDENCE
KERR, Josiah	28	Clerk	Loughbrickland
KERR, Joseph	21	Farmer	Hillsborough
KERR, Hamilton	17	Farmer	Hillsborough
McMURDY, John	30	Farmer	Banbridge
McMULLAN, James	28	Farmer	Loughbrickland
CAVART, Robert	36	Labourer	Rathfryland
FULTON, James	22	Labourer	Maghralin
WALKER, Arthur	27	Labourer	Drumore
GORDON, Thomas	28	Labourer	Drumore
WHANY, Robert	28	Farmer	Drumore
SMITH, Robert	21	Labourer	Hillsborough
HANISON, Hu	13	Farmer	Drumore
ROGAN, Paul	30	Labourer	Loughbrickland
McKEE, William	26	Labourer	Mt Stewart
WILLIAMS, Archibald	21	Farmer	Castledawson
BENSON, John	19	Labourer	Near Drumore
PATTERSON, Robert	24	Farmer	Ballindery
PATTERSON, Adam	20	Farmer	Ballindery
DICKSON, John	33	Farmer	Banbridge
BLACK, James	34	Linen Draper	Banbridge
MOONES, James	21	Farmer	Ballinderry
McMURDY, Anthony	44	Farmer	Banbridge
KERR, Elizabeth	49	Spinster	Loughbrickland
KERR, Elizabeth	30	Spinster	Hillsborough
KERR, Sarah	49	Spinster	Hillsborough
CAVART, Margaret	28	Spinster	Rathfriland
WALKER, Eliza	24	Spinster	Dromore
GORDON, Margaret	21	Spinster	Dromore
WALKER, Margaret	25	Spinster	Hillsborough
WHANY, Jane	35	Spinster	Dromore
WILLIAMS, Nancy	23	Spinster	Castledawson
DICKSON, Jane	21	Spinster	Banbridge
BROWN, Hamilton	35	Farmer	Killinchy
BROWN, Jane	35	Spinster	Killinchy
JAMESON, Jane	50	Spinster	Killinchy
WHALY, William (a child)	7		

SHIP:	MARIA		TO:	Philadelphia
SAIL DATE:	15 March 1804		FROM:	Londonderry

NAME	AGE	OCCUPATION	RESIDENCE
MILLER, William	33	Master	
McCORKELL, Thomas	29	Mate	
WOODS, William	28	2nd Mate	
CASSIN, Joseph	30	Seaman	
MEARES, Thomas	21	Seaman	
GRAY, Guy	24	Seaman	
HOOD, Hugh	31	Seaman	
WILLIAMS, Benjamin	22	Seaman	
FREDD, William	19	Seaman	
WOODS, James	37	Seaman	
GRAY, Robert	25	Seaman	
LAWSON, John	35	Seaman	
JOHNS, William	20	Cook	
McKEEVER, Nancy	45	Spinster	
FULTON, Robert	43	Labourer	
RICE, John	38	Labourer	
HAMMOND, Mary Ann	27	Spinster	
FULTON, Nancy	31	Spinster	
MILLAR, Robert	26	Labourer	
MURPHY, Arthur	49	Labourer	
DOUGHERTY, James	33	Labourer	
McKINLEY, James	23	Labourer	
MURPHY, Sarah	21	Labourer	
McGOMERY, Mary	17	Labourer	
PEARSON, Margaret	52	Spinster	
SCOTT, Francis	47	Labourer	
DOUGHERTY, James	57	Labourer	
McKINLY, Samuel	33	Labourer	
KARLIN, Patt	42	Labourer	
McCONWAY, John	29	Labourer	
McCONWAY, Mary	26	Spinster	
SMITH, Hugh	44	Labourer	
GRAHAM, Humphry	50	Labourer	
GRAHAM, Thomas	36	Labourer	
McCANNA, Barry	43	Labourer	
LEONARD, Robert	21	Labourer	
RANKIN, Henry	17	Labourer	
ANDERSON, William	53	Labourer	
EDMOND, William	41	Labourer	
ANDERSON, John	28	Labourer	
ANDERSON, Henry	46	Labourer	
HARKIN, William	25	Labourer	
ARSKINE, Jos.	56	Labourer	
WAKER, James	40	Labourer	
BELLMAN, Samuel	33	Labourer	
BELLMAN, John	35	Labourer	
ANDERSON, Samuel	46	Labourer	
ANDERSON, Margaret	36	Spinster	
WALKER, Ann	24	Spinster	

| SHIP: | CHARLES AND HARRIOT | | TO: New York |
| SAIL DATE: 3 April 1804 | | | FROM: Sligo |

NAME	AGE	OCCUPATION	RESIDENCE
CARNEY, Martin		Labourer	Mogherow
CARROLL, Peter		Labourer	Mogherow
CURRY, William		Labourer	Conought
McGOWAN, Francis		Clerk	Mogherow
GILL, Roger		Labourer	Co Fermanagh
McMANUS, Bryan		Labourer	Co Fermanagh
ROGERS, Philip		Labourer	Sligo
MUNS, Robert		Labourer	Drumclief
RUTLEDGE, Alexander		Labourer	Tyreragh
MURRY, Hugh		Clerk	Sligo
MORETON, William		Labourer	Co Fermanagh
McINTIRE, Thomas		Clerk	Sligo
COLLEN, Bryan		Labourer	Brenduff
FLYNN, John		Labourer	Drumcliff
GOLDEN, Michael		Labourer	Drumclief
ELLIOTT, John		Labourer	Mullaghmore
DUNN, Michael		Labourer	Mullaghmore
McGARRY, Peter		Labourer	Coloony
O'HARA, Michael		Labourer	Co Sligo
O'HARA, James		Labourer	Co Sligo
O'HARA, Edward		Labourer	Co Sligo
FARRELL, Payton		Labourer	Boyle
FOX, Patt		Labourer	Boyle
McGOWAN, Mark		Labourer	Carney
McGOWAN, Thomas		Labourer	Carney
HART, Con		Labourer	Co Fermanagh
McMORROW, James		Labourer	Sligo
MARTIN, Alexander		Labourer	Sligo
CHAMBERS, William		Labourer	Co Leitrim
CHAMBERS, Edward		Labourer	Co Leitrim

SHIP:	AMERICAN		TO:	New York
SAIL DATE:	3 April 1804		FROM:	Londonderry

NAME	AGE	OCCUPATION	RESIDENCE
SUTHERLAND, David	36	First mate	New York
NESBITT, Robert	20	Second mate	New York
FLEMING, John	30	Mariner	Maryland
BLAKE, William	28	Mariner	Massachusetts
DYSART, James	25	Mariner	New York
COCHRAN, James	30	Mariner	New York
RALSTON, Richard	28	Mariner	New York
ALLRIDGE, George	17	Apprentice	New York
DOUGHERTY, William	16	Apprentice	New York
HAMPHY, James	14	Apprentice	New York
BLAKE, James	40	Cook	New York
ENRING, John	40	Stewart	New York
McKAY, Patrick	40	Farmer	Maghera
McKAY, Alexander	21	Farmer	Maghera
McKAY, Nancy	40		Maghera
BRADLEY, Thomas	20	Farmer	Maghera
DOUGHERTY, John	20	Farmer	Ballyarlin
PARKS, James	28	Gentleman	Bushbank
McGOMERY, Thomas	19	Clerk	Londonderry
STERLING, Captain	25	Mariner	New York
BOND, James	18	Clerk	Londonderry
CLYDE, John	13	Servant	Bushbank
CRAWFORD, George	19	Farmer	Newtown Coningham
JOHNSTON, Robert	20	Farmer	Cumber
RAMSAY, Thomas	21	Farmer	Ballyarnet
IRVINE, Gerard	23	Farmer	Newtonstewart
McGLENEHY, Owen	34	Labourer	Cumber
McGLENEHY, Mary	32		Cumber
DONAGHY, John	41	Labourer	Ennishowin
DOUGHERTY, James	39	Labourer	Newtown Limavady
DOUGHERTY, Eleanor	38		Newtown Limavady
PATTERSON, James	25	Farmer	Desertmartin
McDONALD, Alexander	19	Labourer	Moneymore
RAMSAY, Hugh	29	Labourer	Moneymore
RAMSAY, Alexander	23	Labourer	Moneymore
DOUGHERTY, James	29	Farmer	Moneymore
DONAGHY, William	48	Farmer	Moneymore
DONAGHY, John	19	Farmer	Moneymore
DONAGHY, Alexander	24	Farmer	Moneymore
DONAGHY, Sarah	39	Farmer	Moneymore
McLOUGHLIN, William	50	Farmer	Carn
McLOUGHLIN, John	28	Farmer	Carn
McLOUGHLIN, Alexander	25	Farmer	Carn
McLOUGHLIN, Mary	48	Farmer	Carn
BUCHANNON, James	35	Labourer	Carn
MILLER, William	28	Servant	Newtown Limavady
DOUGHERTY, Alen	35	Labourer	Magilligan

SHIP:	ALEXIS	TO:	Wilmington, North Carolina
SAIL DATE:	3 April 1804	FROM:	Newry

NAME	AGE	OCCUPATION	RESIDENCE
McNIGHT, Hu	40	Farmer	Near Belfast
McNIGHT, James	54	Farmer	Near Belfast
McNIGHT, Batty Snr.	36	Farmer	Near Belfast
McNIGHT, Margaret		Farmer	Near Belfast
McNIGHT, John	3	A child	Near Belfast
McNIGHT, Batty Jnr.	2	A child	Near Belfast
McNIGHT, Eliza	4	A child	Near Belfast
FLANGAN, James		Labourer	Dundalk
GORDON, James		Farmer	Dundalk
WILSON, Hu		Farmer	Dundalk
WILSON, Eliza			Dundalk
GORMAN, Thomas		Labourer	Creggans
GREYSON, William		Labourer	Creggans
PLUNKET, Oliver		Labourer	Creggans
MACKEY, Michael		Labourer	Cullaville
MURPHY, Terence		Labourer	Carrickmacross
VANCE, William		Labourer	Carrickmacross
TRENOR, Patrick		Labourer	Carrickmacross
ALLISON, William		Master	
HUTCHESON, William		1st Mate	
SIMPSON, George		2nd Mate	
McCLEAN, Neil		Mariner	
THOMPSON, Robert		Mariner	
McDOUGAL, John		Apprentice	
MORRISON, Daniel		Apprentice	
EDMONSTON, John		Apprentice	
MAGOWEN, Dugal		Mariner	
GRAHAM, Samuel		Mariner	
SAVAGE, Rowland		Mariner	

NAME	AGE	OCCUPATION	RESIDENCE
JEFFERS, William		Farmer	Loghadill
GRIFFITH, Alexander		Farmer	Loghadill
HODMAN, John		Farmer	Loghadill
TAYLOR, George		Labourer	Loghadill
GRIFFITH, Robert		Labourer	Loghadill
LAW, John		Labourer	Moghean
ELLIOTT, Robert		Labourer	Moghean
ELLIOTT, Archibald		Labourer	Moghean
ELLIS, David		Farmer	Tillon
ARMSTRONG, Thomas		Farmer	Tillon
TAYLOR, Andrew		Labourer	Tillon
YOUNG, George		Labourer	Tillon
FARRELL, Michael		Labourer	Tillon
McMORROW, John		Labourer	Cloghfin
BRADY, Peter		Labourer	Cloghfin
CARTY, John		Labourer	Ardnastraw
McDONOGH, Patt		Labourer	Ardnastraw
McNOSSEN, Andrew		Clerk	Ardnastraw
DONOGHER, Michael		Labourer	Ardnastraw
DONOGHER, James		Labourer	Ardnastraw
McDONOGHER Jun.		Labourer	Ardnastraw
CRAIG, Robert		Labourer	Loughfin
CRAWFORD, Edward		Labourer	Loughfin
CAFFRY, Ben		Labourer	Loughfin
CAFFUNY, James		Labourer	Loughfin
VAUGH, William		Clerk	Loughfin
DOWLER, Henry		Clerk	Barton
DUFFY, John		Labourer	Barton
CRAWFORD, Hugh		Labourer	Barton
PATTERSON, Thomas		Labourer	Barton
DAVIS, Hugh		Labourer	Barton

SHIP:	SUSAN	TO:	New York
SAIL DATE:	3 April 1804	FROM:	Dublin

NAME	AGE	OCCUPATION	RESIDENCE
GLENNING, Patrick	22	Labourer	Monastereven, Co Kildare
GLENNING, Mary	24	Spinster	Monastereven, Co Kildare
CAWLIN, Michael	23	Labourer	Nober, Co Meath
KENNY, Mary	36	Married	Dublin City
DONOGAN, Edward	21	Labourer	Connotwood, Queens County
BRANGHILL, Michael	30	Labourer	Bala Branghen, Kings County
FULLARD, Eliza	26	Spinster	Edenderry, Kings County
FULLARD, Frances	14	Spinster	Edenderry, Kings County
FULLARD, Jane	10	Spinster	Edenderry, Kings County
CAFFREY, Nicholas	21	Farmer	Monastereven, Co Kildare
WOGAN, Patrick	20	Gentleman	Dublin City
RHIND, Good	23	Gentleman	Dublin City
CARRILL, Keeron	23	Servant	Dublin City
DURM, Thomas	28	Labourer	Bala Branaghan, Kings County
TAYLOR, Michael	38	Labourer	Dublin City
MEATLAND, Thomas	21	Labourer	Dunlavan, Co Wicklow
MEATLAND, Anne	56	Married	Dunlavan, Co Wicklow
MEATLAND, Mary Anne	20	Spinster	Dunlavan, Co Wicklow
BARRY, James	23	Gentleman	Dublin City
McDERMOTT, Edward	30	Gentleman	Dublin City
DYAS, Robert	19	Gentleman	Kings Court, Co Cavan
GORE, James	26	Gentleman	Dublin City
YATES, James	34	Gentleman	Newry Town
DEMPSEY, Joseph	18	Servant	Upper Wood, Queens County
CAMPBELL, Judith	25	Married	Knockmack, Co Meath
HYNES, Jane	30	Married	Drogheda, Co Meath
KELLY, Mark	30	Farmer	Monastereven, Co Kildare
KELLY, Mary	30	Married	Monastereven, Co Kildare
FORAN, John	35	Labourer	Monastereven, Co Kildare
DONNOLLY, Simon	22	Labourer	Naas, Co Kildare
TOOLE, Luke	28	Clerk	Donnybrook, Co Dublin
CHRISTIAN, William	25	Labourer	Dublin City
HOBART, Nicholas	30	Labourer	Mullingar, Co Meath
MURTHES, Michael	25	Labourer	Lurgangreen, Co Louth

| SHIP: | BROTHERS | | TO: | Philadelphia |
| SAIL DATE: | 17 April 1804 | | FROM: | Londonderry |

NAME	AGE	OCCUPATION	RESIDENCE
FULLERTON, James	28	Mate	
McAVOY, William	24	2nd mate	
FERNANDEZ, Joshua	30	Seaman	
BUTTER, Peter	24	Seaman	
MACK, Anthony	34	Seaman	
GRIGGS, Daniel	28	Seaman	
BENFORD, William	17	Seaman	
ROLPH, Charles	17	Seaman	
WHITE, John	34	Cook	
MAGE, Samuel	29	Stewart	
OSBURN, Margaret	27	Spinster	Omagh, Co Tyrone
THOMPSON, John	23	Farmer	Castlefin, Co Donegal
KEARNEY, Ann	35	Spinster	Dungiven, Co Derry
KEARNEY, Patrick	12	A child	Dungiven, Co Derry
KEARNEY, John	9	A child	Dungiven, Co Derry
KEARNEY, Biddy	7	A child	Dungiven, Co Derry
KEARNEY, Nancy	4	A child	Dungiven, Co Derry
YOUNG, Noble	23	Farmer	Pettigow, Co Fermanagh
YOUNG, James	21	Labourer	Pettigow, Co Fermanagh
YOUNG, Sarah	50	Spinster	Pettigow, Co Fermanagh
HIBRAN, James	30	Labourer	Castlefin, Co Donegal
HIBRAN, Jos	22	Labourer	Castlefin, Co Donegal
HUNTON, Jane	35	Spinster	Castlefin, Co Donegal
BOYD, James	26	Farmer	Pettigo, Co Fermanagh
WISHART, Margaret	21	Spinster	Pettigo, Co Fermanagh
WISHART, James	51	Labourer	Dungannon, Co Tyrone
KELLY, Charles	21	Labourer	Drummore, Co Tyrone
KELLY, Hugh	22	Labourer	Drummore, Co Tyrone
OSBURN, Margaret	27	Spinster	Omagh, Co Tyrone
OSBURN, Jane	6	Child	Omagh, Co Tyrone
OSBURN, James	4	Child	Omagh, Co Tyrone
FLANIGAN, Charles	34	Labourer	Ballyshannon, Co Donegal
FLANIGAN, Mary	28	Spinster	Ballyshannon, Co Donegal
FLANIGAN, John	8	Child	Ballyshannon, Co Donegal
KELLY, Hu	30	Labourer	Ballyshannon, Co Donegal
KANE, John	24	Labourer	Ballyshannon, Co Donegal
BOYLE, James	40	Labourer	Ballyshannon, Co Donegal
ROBINSON, William	32	Labourer	Coleraine, Co Derry
ROBINSON, Ann	22	Spinster	Innishannon, Co Donegal
DOHERTY, John	30	Labourer	Innishannon, Co Donegal
DOHERTY, Mary	26	Spinster	Innishannon, Co Donegal
McLOUGHLIN, Patt	32	Labourer	Innishannon, Co Donegal
McLOUGHLIN, R	24	Labourer	Innishannon, Co Donegal
DOHERTY, William	23	Labourer	Innishannon, Co Donegal
DOHERTY, James	28	Farmer	Beet, Co Donegal
DUNN, James	24	Farmer	Beet, Co Donegal
DUNN, Mary	19	Spinster	Beet, Co Donegal
PORTER, James	35	Farmer	Beet, Co Donegal

SHIP: FOLLANSLER   TO: Baltimore

SAIL DATE: 17 April 1804   FROM: Belfast

NAME	AGE	OCCUPATION	RESIDENCE
GIBSON, Robert	28	Farmer	Dromon, Co Down
GIBSON, Sarah	27		Dromon, Co Down
GIBSON, Mary	60		Hillsborough, Co Down
GIBSON, John	30	Farmer	Hillsborough, Co Down
GIBSON, David	28	Farmer	Hillsborough, Co Down
GIBSON, Ann	20		Hillsborough, Co Down
GIBSON, Elizabeth	18		Hillsborough, Co Down
TAGGART, Jane	40		Dromon, Co Down
TAGGART, Anne	14		Dromon, Co Down
TAGGART, Jane	12		Dromon, Co Down
COTTER, William	28	Labourer	Ballymona, Co Antrim
COTTER, Ann	26		Ballymona, Co Antrim
DIVINE, Felix	38	Dealer	Philadelphia, America
NESBIT, Robert	40	Dealer	Killinchy, Co Down
McCAUSLAND, James	30	Farmer	Cookstown, Co Tyrone
McCAUSLAND, Susanna	28		Cookstown, Co Tyrone
RICHARDSON, Alexander	28	Dealer	Baltimore, America
RICHARDSON, Mary Ann	24		Baltimore, America
GREER, William	25	Dealer	Baltimore, America
CLELAND, James	24	Dealer	Ballynillon, Co Down
CLELAND, George	21	Farmer	Ballynillon, Co Down
LINDLEY, William	20	Farmer	Ballynillon, Co Down
LOWRY, Robert	55	Dealer	Killinchwood, Co Down
LOWRY, Mary	55	Dealer	Killinchwood, Co Down
LOWRY, Robert	26	Farmer	Killinchwood, Co Down
LOWRY, James	24	Labourer	Killinchwood, Co Down
LOWRY, William	20	Labourer	Killinchwood, Co Down
LOWRY, Jane	18		Killinchwood, Co Down
HUTTON, George	21	Farmer	Killinchwood, Co Down
DELAP, Francis	50	Farmer	Comber, Co Down
DELAP, Alexander	22	Farmer	Comber, Co Down
DELAP, Jane	50		Comber, Co Down
DELAP, Jane	20		Comber, Co Down
DELAP, Christian	18		Comber, Co Down
MORROW, Andrew	40	Labourer	Ballyargin, Co Down
MORROW, Jane	30		Ballyargin, Co Down
BOYD, Mary	31		Dromon, Co Down
BOYD, Daniel	34	Farmer	Dromon, Co Down

SHIP:	WILLIAM AND JANE		TO: New York
SAIL DATE: 17 April 1804			FROM: Belfast

NAME	AGE	OCCUPATION	RESIDENCE
EATON, John	30	Farmer	Tamlah Parish and Town, Co Derry
EATON, James	28	Farmer	Tamlah Parish and Town, Co Derry
EATON, Samuel	29	Farmer	Tamlah Parish and Town, Co Derry
EATON, Mary	25	Spinster	Tamlah Parish and Town, Co Derry
MAXWELL, Mathew	25	Gentleman	Ballyooly, Rathfryland, Co Down
LOUGHRAN, Robert	23	Labourer	Near Cookstown, Co Tyrone
LOUGHRAN, Bridget	25	Spinster	Near Cookstown, Co Tyrone
LUNDY, John	34	Farmer	Near Tandragee, Co Armagh
HENDERSON, William	21	Farmer	Raloe near Larne, Co Antrim
McKEVY, Philip	25	Farmer	Raloe near Larne, Co Antrim
ROBB, Alexander	24	Labourer	Broadisland Parish, Co Antrim
ALEXANDER, William	20	Labourer	Broadisland Parish, Co Antrim
BROWN, Widow	60	Spinster	Parish of Killileagh, Co Down
BROWN, William	20	Farmer	Parish of Killileagh, Co Down
BROWN, Margaret	25	Spinster	Parish of Killileagh, Co Down
BROWN, Barbara	18	Spinster	Parish of Killileagh, Co Down
McCULLOH, John	21	Labourer	Parish of Drumbo, Co Down
WITHERS, Margaret	25	Spinster	Parish of Drumbo, Co Down
ROBISON, John	28	Labourer	Near Porlavo Archin Parish, Co Down
STEEN, John	13	Labourer	Near Coan, Co Antrim
BURNS, John	30	Labourer	Drumgolan near Rathfryland, Co Down
DOYLE, Denis	34	Labourer	Drumgolan near Rathfryland, Co Down
DOYLE, Margaret	34	Spinster	Drumgolan, near Rathfryland, Co Down
DOYLE, Michael	27	Labourer	Drumgolan, near Rathfryland, Co Down
DOYLE, Eliza	27	Spinster	Drumgolan, near Rathfryland, Co Down
O'NEAL, Arthur	23	Farmer	Near Castlereagh, Co Down
MORRISON, Samuel	27	Farmer	Parish of Killinchy, Co Down
MORRISON, Mary	25	Spinster	Parish of Killinchy, Co Down
RUSK, James	23	Farmer	Derriaghy near Lisburn, Co Antrim
McCRAY, George	20	Farmer	Dunerisk near Cookstown, Co Tyrone

SHIP:	JUNO	TO:	New York
SAIL DATE:	17 April 1804	FROM:	Dublin

NAME	AGE	OCCUPTION	RESIDENCE
MERRIHEW, Stephen		Master	
ELDRIDGE, Isaiah		Mate	
SOALE, James		Mate	
STACKPOLE, Frances		Seaman	
FULD, Alexander		Seaman	
WALKER, Curtes		Seaman	
CALLAGHAN, Richard		Seaman	
BEACHMAN, John		Seaman	
DINNAMON, John		Seaman	
TRUEMAN, John		Cook	
CRANMER, John		Apprentice	
HORNRIDGE, James	26	Surgeon	Britain Street
HORNRIDGE, Mary	19		Britain Street
HALLERAN, George	34	Clerk	Britain Street
HALLERAN, Jane	26		Britain Street
DARTNELL, Edward	27	Clerk	Britain Street
CORISH, Catherine	32		James Street
CORISH, Miss	8		James Street
SMITH, Michael	24	Farmer	Cleghan, Co Cavan
MULLAHY, John	22	Farmer	Callan, Co Kilkenny
HULLY, John	35	Farmer	Callan, Co Kilkenny
TENNING, Denis	25	Farmer	Callan, Co Kilkenny
MAHER, Thomas	24	Farmer	Callan, Co Kilkenny
MAHER, Mary	22		Callan, Co Kilkenny
Infant child			Callan, Co Kilkenny
CORMACK, Patrick	17	Farmer	Callan, Co Kilkenny
CARTY, William	17	Farmer	Callan, Co Kilkenny
WHITE, Alice	50		Boston, AN
WHITE, Catherine	22		Callan, Co Kilkenny
WHITE, Mary	20		Callan, Co Kilkenny
WHITE, Eleanor	18		Callan, Co Kilkenny
CORMICK, Margaret	20		Callan, Co Kilkenny
ROSSETER, John	22	Farmer	Wexford
ROSSETER, James	24	Farmer	Wexford
BAHAN, Thomas	26	Clerk	Bride Street

SHIP:	MARY			TO:	Philadelphia
SAIL DATE:	17 April 1804			FROM:	Dublin

NAME	AGE	OCCUPATION	RESIDENCE
COGGESHALL, James		Master	
CRASS, Earl		Mate	
COOK, Charles		Mate	
COGGESHALL, Charles		Seaman	
HOUSTON, Arthur		Seaman	
SUMLAND, Samuel		Seaman	
SMITH, James		Seaman	
JOHNSON, Peter		Seaman	
NELIS, Peter		Seaman	
DAVES, Richard		Apprentice	
COTTER, George		Apprentice	
CHICK, William		Apprentice	
FILE, Richard	50	Merchant	Philadelphia
KINNEY, Patrick	39	Clergyman	Lush, Co Dublin
BAINBRIDGE, James R	20	Clerk	Bridge Street,
CASSIDY, Lawrence	25	Clerk	Coombe
STONE, Oliver W	22	Clerk	Lurgan, Co Armagh
HUDSON, Elizabeth	22		Grafton Street
MULHOLLAN, Anne	17		Ballycumber, Kings County
GORDON, Miss	17		Philadelphia
COOGAN, William	40	Farmer	Pensylvania
FAGAN, James	30	Farmer	Wrath, Queens County
McCARTY, James	25	Farmer	Wexford
BYRNE, Henry	30	Farmer	Wexford
GARTER, Owen	26	Farmer	Wrath
POWER, William	28	Farmer	Fothered, Co Tipperary
DAILY, Mathew	25	Farmer	Killkullen, Co Kildare
DAILY, Thomas	23	Farmer	Killkullen, Co Kildare
GORMAN, Edward	35	Farmer	Rushall, Queens County
BOYER, Mathew	30	Labourer	Kildare
DAILY, Catherine	22		Kilkullen
GOTHAN, William	10	Child	Dublin
FAGAN, Mary	25		Mt Rath
DICKINSON, Robert	30	Farmer	Wicklow
DICKINSON, Rose	25		Wicklow
KAGAN, Patrick	30	Farmer	Borris in Apory
ROYDON, Anthony	25	Farmer	Borris in Apory
PORTER, Ann Field	20		Dublin

NAME	AGE	OCCUPATION	RESIDENCE
LYNCH, Edward	22	Labourer	Armagh
FRANCES, Robert	30	Farmer	Cavan
FRANCES, Jane	28		Cavan
FRANCES, Mary	2		Cavan
FARLEY, Margaret	20		Cavan
GILMOR, William	54	Labourer	Cavan
GILMORE, Jane	50		Cavan
GILMOR, Frances	21		Cavan
GILMOR, James	19	Labourer	Cavan
GILMOR, Rose	17		Cavan
GILMOR, Jourdan	16		Cavan
HART, Bartley	17		Cavan
McQUILLAN, Andrew	40	Farmer	Cavan
McMULLEN, Margaret	41		Cavan
McMULLEN, John	20	Farmer	Cavan
McMULLEN, William	18	Labourer	Cavan
McQUILLEN, Agnes	16		Cavan
McMULLEN, Samuel	13		Cavan
WRIGHT, William	40	Labourer	Cavan
FERGUSON, David	54	Labourer	Armagh
FERGUSON, Robert	25	Farmer	Down
FERGUSON, William	21	Farmer	Down
FERGUSON, Hugh	19	Farmer	Down
FERGUSON, James	16	Farmer	Down
FERGUSON, Eliza	14		Down
McBRIDE, James	37	Farmer	Down
McBRIDGE, William	22	Farmer	Down
McBRIDE, Sarah	10		Down
LARD, James	30	Farmer	Armagh
LARD, Margaret	31		Armagh
LARD, Jane	8		Armagh
LARD, Sarah	2		Armagh
MURPHY, James	36	Farmer	Armagh
MURPHY, Mary	30		Armagh
MURPHY, James	5		Armagh
WHELDON, Joseph		Master	
SITH, Joby		First Mate	
MASON, Richard		2nd Mate	
KIBTON, Hanamiah		Mariner	
ALLEN, Eleser		Mariner	
CROKER, James		Mariner	
BROWN, Jourdan		Mariner	
BROWN, James		Mariner	
SMITH, John		Mariner	
MORGAN, Michael		Mariner	
DELINE, Nathan		Mariner	

NAME	AGE	OCCUPATION	RESIDENCE
JELLY, Hugh	35	Labourer	Loughinisland Parish, Co Down
THOMSON, Hugh	36	Labourer	Kilmore Parish, Co Down
LINDSEY, Joseph	33	Labourer	Sea Patrick, Co Down
BECK, James	30	Farmer	Ashegarg Parish, Co Down
BECK, John	25	Farmer	Ashegarg Parish, Co Down
BECK, Margaret	24	Spinster	Ashegarg Parish, Co Down
KILPATRICK, Thomas	37	Farmer	Killead Parish, Co Antrim
CUNNINGHAM, Patt	30	Farmer	Loughinisland Parish, Co Down
MITCHELL, Sarah	25	Spinster	Loughinisland Parish, Co Down
McGOWAN, William	35	Farmer	Dunmurry, Co Antrim
GORDON, John	36	Farmer	Keady Parish, Co Armagh
DINWIDDIE, William	40	Farmer	Dunaghy Parish, Co Antrim
LOGAN, George	30	Labourer	Killinchy Parish, Co Down
LOGAN, George Jun	25	Labourer	Killinchy Parish, Co Down
McCAUGHTRY, Robert	25	Farmer	Carnmoney Parish, Co Antrim
McCAUGHTRY, Jane	30	Spinster	Carnmoney Parish, Co Antrim
DICKEY, Isaac	20	Farmer	Magheragill Parish, Co Down
STEWART, Anne	18	Spinster	Belfast, Co Antrim
STEVENSON, Thomas	21	Farmer	Dunaghy Parish, Co Antrim
DOUGLASS, John	42	Farmer	Seaford Parish, Co Down
DOUGLASS, Mary	38	Spinster	Seaford Parish, Co Down
McAFEE, Agniss	20	Spinster	Belfast, Co Antrim
MARTIN, George	35	Farmer	Blaris Parish, Co Down
SHERRY, John	34	Farmer	Blaris Parish, Co Down
McCARROLL, Patrick	26	Farmer	Augher Parish, Co Tyrone
DUROSS, John	21	Farmer	Dublin, Co Dublin
O'NEILL, Francis	27	Labourer	Dublin, Co Dublin
O'NEILL, Emelia	22	Spinster	Dublin, Co Dublin
COURTNEY, Richard	25	Farmer	Clough Parish, Co Down
COURTNEY, Margaret	24	Spinster	Clough Parish, Co Down
BAILIE, Mathew	48	Farmer	Clough Parish, Co Down
BAILIE, Eliza	46	Spinster	Clough Parish, Co Down
BAILIE, Stewart	20	Farmer	Clough Parish, Co Down
BAILIE, Matty	18	Spinster	Clough Parish, Co Down
FERRIS, William	25	Farmer	Ballymina, Co Antrim
FERRIS, Anne	32	Spinster	Ballymina, Co Antrim
His wife			

NAME	AGE	OCCUPATION	RESIDENCE
DESPARD, Richard	35	Merchant	New York, America
DESPARD, Mary	28	Merchant	Mew York, America
McANNALLY, James	47	Merchant	No 3 Old Merrion, Dublin
TAYLOR, Thomas	25	Farmer	Ballywater, Co Wexford
BERFORD, William	19	Farmer	Ballywater, Co Wexford
BRICE, Thomas	24	Labourer	Dublin
BRICE, Hanora	17	Labourer	Dublin
DOLAND, Mary	26	Servant to Mrs Despard	Mountrath
REYNOLDS, George	50	Farmer	St Margaret, Dublin
REYNOLDS, Mary	40		St Margaret, Dublin
REYNOLDS, Johnathan	9		St Margaret, Dublin
REYNOLDS, Thomas	7		St Margaret, Dublin
REYNOLDS, Eliza	5		St Margaret, Dublin
DAVISON, William	28	Farmer	Leiterbeag, Co Cavan
DAVISON, Mary	28	Farmer	Leiterbeag, Co Cavan
DAVISON, William	5		Leiterbeag, Co Cavan
DAVISON, Edward	4		Leiterbeag, Co Cavan
BROWN, Easter	20	Servant to Mrs Davison	Leiterbeag, Co Cavan
McMULLIN, Betsey	60	Servant to Mrs Davison	Caverhalman, Co Cavan
McMULLIN, Jane	28	Servant to Mrs Davison	Caverhalman, Co Cavan
McMULLIN, Fanny	18	Servant to Mrs Davison	Caverhalman, Co Cavan
SHIELDS, Henry	30	Farmer	Kings Court, Co Cavan
SHIELDS, Ann	29	Farmer	Kings Court, Co Cavan
HIGGINS, James	27	Farmer	Caverhalman, Co Cavan
BRADY, John	27	Farmer	Caverhalman, Co Cavan
McMULLIN, John	50	Farmer	Pattle, Co Cavan
McMULLIN, Mary	50		Pattle, Co Cavan
McMULLIN, Jonathan	20	Farmer	Pattle, Co Cavan
McMULLIN, William	18	Farmer	Pattle, Co Cavan
McMULLIN, Thomas	16	Farmer	Pattle, Co Cavan
McMULLIN, Andrew	13	Farmer	Pattle, Co Cavan
McMULLIN, Easter	9	Farmer	Pattle, Co Cavan
McMULLIN, Alexander	22	Farmer	Pattle, Co Cavan
McMULLIN, Barbara	22	Farmer	Pattle, Co Cavan
REDMOND, Patrick	47	Farmer	Baley, Co Wexford
REDMOND, Bridget	35	Farmer	Baley, Co Wexford
REDMOND, Jonathan	12	Farmer	Baley, Co Wexford
REDMOND, Nicholas	10	Farmer	Baley, Co Wexford
REDMOND, Elizabeth	7	Farmer	Baley, Co Wexford
REDMOND, Bridget	5	Farmer	Baley, Co Wexford

SHIP:	SERPENT		TO:	Baltimore
SAIL DATE:	8 May 1803		FROM:	Londonderry

NAME	AGE	OCCUPATION	RESIDENCE
KING, John	37	1st Mate	Baltimore
STYLES, John	27	2nd Mate	Baltimore
BENTON, Thomas	22	Mariner	Baltimore
GALBRAITH, James	30	Mariner	Baltimore
AVERY, Charles	21	Mariner	Baltimore
FRESCHMOLLER, Hanibal	24	Mariner	Bergen
LYND, Henry	32	Mariner	Sweeden
PLATT, George	19	Apprentice Mariner	Baltimore
COCHRAN, Charles	24	Farmer	Fermanagh
COCHRAN, Elizabeth	24	Spinster	Fermanagh
COCHRAN, Henry	3	Child	Fermanagh
IRVIN, John	21	Farmer	Drumhiny
IRVIN, Charlotte	45	Spinster	Drumhiny
McGEE, Andrew	21	Farmer	Killygordon
BRANDON, William	21	Labourer	Crumlin
BRANDON, Henry	20	Labourer	Crumlin
BRANDON, Gerard	18	Labourer	Crumlin
BRANDON, James	16	Farmer	Crumlin
BRANDON, John	14	Labourer	Crumlin
BRANDON, Mary	18	Spinster	Crumlin
BRANDON, Edward	15	Labourer	Crumlin
BRANDON, Isabella	10	Spinster	Crumlin
BRANDON, Christopher	8	Child	Crumlin
BRANDON, Mary	40	Spinster	Crumlin
BRANDON, Thomas	4	Child	Crumlin
BRANDON, Jane	6	Child	Crumlin
McCAUSLAND, Oliver	22	Farmer	Omagh
HARVEY, Thomas	22	Farmer	Omagh
DAVIS, James	26	Farmer	Dungannon
DAVIS, Margaret	25	Spinster	Dungannon
SCOTT, Samuel	60	Farmer	Cosquin
SCOTT, Ann	69	Spinster	Cosquin
SCOTT, Rebecca	30	Spinster	Cosquin
SCOTT, Frances	22	Spinster	Cosquin
SCOTT, Ann	20	Spinster	Cosquin
SCOTT, Samuel	28	Farmer	Cosquin
CARTER, Jane	30	Spinster	Cosquin
CARTER, John	35	Farmer	Cosquin
JOHNSTON, John	22	Farmer	Ardstraw
McCOLLEY, James	19	Labourer	Linamore
JOHNSTON, Stephen	21	Labourer	Adderny
BALL, John	36	Farmer	Leighan
BALL, Prudence	30	Spinster	Leighan
BALL, Edward	14	Labourer	Leighan
BALL, John	12	Labourer	Leighan
DOHERTY, John	21	Farmer	Clonmany
DOHERTY, George	21	Farmer	Clonmany

SHIP:	SALLY	TO:	New York
SAIL DATE:	15 May 1804	FROM:	Newry

NAME	AGE	OCCUPATION	RESIDENCE
CLIFTON, Timothy			
HOLE, William			
CAMERON, John			
MARTIN, John			
DEAL, James			
WHITE, Hugh			
BROWN, John			
REED, Moses			
McBERNEY, William	35	Farmer	Dramary Parish, Co Down
McBERNEY, Alice	32		Dramary Parish, Co Down
Three Children	5		Dramary Parish, Co Down
KELLY, David	36	Farmer	Dramary Parish, Co Down
KELLY, Mary	36		Dramary Parish, Co Down
Six Children	10		Dramary Parish, Co Down
MARTIN, Eliza	30		Killevey, Co Armagh
McCRUM, James	30	Farmer	Tynan, Co Armagh
McCRUM, Sarah	30		Tynan, Co Armagh
Two Children	4		Tynan, Co Armagh
STEWART, Michael	18	Labourer	Tynan, Co Armagh
FAMISTER, John	30	Farmer	Armagh Parish, Co Armagh
FAMISTER, Ann	22		Armagh Parish, Co Armagh
FAMISTER, Jane	25		Armagh Parish, Co Armagh
KINMAC, Robert	25	Labourer	Keady, Co Armagh

SHIP:	JEFFERSON	TO:	Newcastle and Philadelphia
SAIL DATE:	15 May 1804	FROM:	Ballyshannon

NAME	AGE	OCCUPATION	RESIDENCE
MAGUIRE, Francis	38	Labourer	Barony of Lurg, Co Fermanagh
MAGUIRE, Bridget	36		Barony of Lurg, Co Fermanagh
THOMPSON, Edward	34	Labourer	Barony of Lurg, Co Fermanagh
THOMPSON, John	24	Labourer	Barony of Lurg, Co Fermanagh
THOMPSON, Mary	22		Barony of Lurg, Co Fermanagh
THOMPSON, Edward Jun	8		Barony of Lurg, Co Fermanagh
CONOLLY, Patt	33	Labourer	Resinver, Co Leitrim
CONOLLY, Rose	31		Resinver, Co Leitrim
STEPHENSON, Charles	29	Farmer	Tirehugh, Co Donegal
STEPHENSON, John	27	Farmer	Tirehugh, Co Donegal
STEPHENSON, Margaret	22		Tirehugh, Co Donegal
DIVER, Thomas	25	Chapman	Tirehugh, Co Donegal
DIVER, Mary	26		Tirehugh, Co Donegal
JOHNSTON, Robert	15	Clerk	Donegal, Co Donegal
STEPHENSON, William	20	Farmer	Donegal, Co Donegal
CONNOR, John	20	Labourer	Drumcliffe, Co Sligo
CULLIN, Francis	16	Labourer	Resinver, Co Leitrim
McPARTLAN, Hugh	23	Labourer	Ballyshannon
McPARTLAN, Mary	22		Ballyshannon
TIFFANY, Daniel	24	Labourer	Resinver, Co Leitrim
KNIGHT, Daniel six seamen & one cook			Citizens of USA

NAME	AGE	OCCUPATION	RESIDENCE
McCLENACHAN, Johnston	40	Master	
ROBINSON, John	40	Mate	
WILLIAMS, Edward	23	Mariner	
HISLAN, James	24	Mariner	
LAWRENCE, James	22	Mariner	
SMITH, David	22	Mariner	
DAVIDSON, John	24	Mariner	
EVAN, David	27	Mariner	
SWAN, Thomas	20	Mariner	
JACKSON, Thomas	25	Mariner	
ROBINSON, James	30	Mariner	
SMITH, James	35	Mariner	
CRAWFORD, James	45	Farmer	Kinnaty
ROBINSON, John	40	Farmer	Omagh
ROBINSON, Jane	36	Farmer	Omagh
ROBINSON, Robert	20	Farmer	Omagh
ROBINSON, Joseph	18	Labourer	Omagh
ROBINSON, James	11	Labourer	Omagh
ROBINSON, John	16	Labourer	Omagh
ROBINSON, Mary	7	Spinster	Omagh
ROBINSON, Barber	5	Spinster	Omagh
ROBINSON, Ann	3	Spinster	Omagh
MILLS, Henry	35	Farmer	Ballogrey
FULTON, James	30	Farmer	Omagh
McNAMEE, Patrick	25	Labourer	Augher
GRAY, Joseph	40	Farmer	Augher
DOHERTY, Hugh Sen	38	Laborer	Augher
DOHERTY, Hugh Jun	16	Labourer	Augher
DOHERTY, John	14	Labourer	Augher
DOHERTY, Unity	32	Spinster	Augher
DOHERTY, Elenor	19	Spinster	Augher
CALDWELL, John	30	Farmer	Augher
CALDWELL, Elizabeth	29	Spinster	Augher
CALDWELL, James	9	Farmer	Augher
CALDWELL, Elizabeth	7	Spinster	Augher
CALDWELL, Jane	17	Spinster	Augher
CALDWELL, Thomas	30	Farmer	Augher
CRAWFORD, John	28	Farmer	Augher
CALDWELL, Elizabeth	29	Spinster	Augher
CALDWELL, Isabella	13	Spinster	Augher
CALDWELL, Joseph	11	Farmer	Augher
CALDWELL, Joseph	9	Farmer	Augher
CALDWELL, Isabella	7	Spinster	Augher
CALDWELL, Alexander	10	Farmer	Augher
CALDWELL, Jane	7	Spinster	Augher
WATT, Joseph	30	Farmer	Augher
McCANNA, Patrick	24	Labourer	Augher
LOWTHER, Joseph	24	Labourer	Augher
QUIN, Thomas	25	Labourer	Hollyhill
DIVIN, Edward	24	Labourer	Hollyhill
HARGAN, James	25	Labourer	Hollyhill
MULHERON, John	26	Labourer	Strabane
GRAY, Sarah	30	Spinster	Newtonstewart
GRAY, Boshall	28	Labourer	Newtonstewart
CROSBY, Neal	24	Labourer	Newtonstewart
RODGERS, John	21	Labourer	Newtonstewart
RODGERS, Robert	23	Labourer	Newtonstewart
McDIVITT, James	24	Labourer	Newtonstewart
IRWINE, William	27	Labourer	Newtonstewart
McMILLAN, Samuel	24	Labourer	Newtonstewart

NAME	AGE	OCCUPATION	RESIDENCE
WILLSON, Robert	24	Labourer	Newtownstewart
McCAY, Robert	24	Labourer	Newtownstewart
REED, John	25	Labourer	Ballindret
HUNTER, Alexander	21	Labourer	Ballindret
HUNTER, Robert	19	Labourer	Ballindret
ROSS, John	26	Labourer	New York
KING, John	32	Labourer	New York
ARMSTRONG, Susanna	38	Spinster	Cams
ARMSTRONG, Mary	23	Spinster	Cams
ARMSTRONG, John	18	Labourer	Cams
ARMSTRONG, Nancy	16	Spinster	Cams
McGUIRE, James	30	Labourer	Cams
GETTY, John	50	Labourer	Faughinvale
GETTY, Abigail	45	Spinster	Faughinvale
GETTY, James	26	Labourer	Faughinvale
ADEMS, Robert	45	Labourer	Faughinvale
ADEMS, Elizabeth	38	Spinster	Faughinvale
ADEMS, John	15	Labourer	Faughinvale
ADEMS, Archibald	12	Labourer	Faughinvale
ADEMS, Mary	10	Spinster	Faughinvale
ADEMS, Elizabeth	8	Spinster	Faughinvale
ADEMS, Martha	6	Spinster	Faughinvale

NAME	AGE	OCCUPATION	RESIDENCE
CLEGG, Benjamin	22	Gentleman	Stradbally, Queens County
CLEGG, George	26	Gentleman	Stradbally, Queens County
RYAN, Revd Mathew	60	Clergyman	Dublin, Co Dublin
CARNEY, James	56	Farmer	Athy, Co Kildare
CARNEY, Mary	50	Farmer	Athy, Co Kildare
CARNEY, Thomas	30	Farmer	Athy, Co Kildare
CARNEY, John	20	Farmer	Athy, Co Kildare
CARNEY, Nicholas	19	Farmer	Athy, Co Kildare
CARNEY, Martin	11	Farmer	Athy, Co Kildare
CARNEY, Elinor	16	Farmer	Athy, Co Kildare
DOBBYN, Ellen	20	Farmer	Stradbally, Queens County
ROGERS, William	30	Gentleman	Dublin, Co Dublin
HAY, John	23	Gentleman	Newry, Co Down
REYNOLDS, George	42	Gentleman	St Margarets, Dublin
REYNOLDS, Mary			St Margarets, Dublin
CHRISTIAN, Mathew	22	Labourer	Borris, Queens County

NAME	AGE	OCCUPATION	RESIDENCE
SHIELDS, James	40	1st Mate	
PAXTON, John	28	2nd Mate	
GRIFFIN, John	22	Seaman	
HALEROW, Henry	21	Seaman	
POTTER, John	36	Cook	
HALEROW, Nicholas	16	Apprentice	
IRWIN, Curwen	15	Apprentice	
SMITH, John	11	Apprentice	
McCAULEY, George	17	Apprentice	
ANGUS, John	12	Apprentice	
CUTHBERT, George	35	Labourer	Coleraine Parish
ALCORN, James	40	Labourer	Glenvenogh Parish, Co Donegal
ALCORN, Michael	16	Labourer	Glenvenogh Parish, Co Donegal
ALCORN, John	17	Labourer	Glenvenogh Parish, Co Donegal
GALLAGHER, Mary	35	Spinster	Glenvenogh Parish, Co Donegal
CUTHBERT, Ann	13	Spinster	Glenvenogh Parish, Co Donegal
CUTHBERT, Fanny	12	Spinster	Glenvenogh Parish, Co Donegal
COYLE, John	20	Farmer	Glenvenogh Parish, Co Donegal
McCARAN, James	20	Farmer	Glenvenogh Parish, Co Donegal
McCARAN, Edward	22	Farmer	Glenvenogh Parish, Co Donegal
TODD, James	19	Labourer	Largilly
GIBSON, John	19	Labourer	Ballycloy
PAUL, Thomas	20	Labourer	Co Down
ELLIOTT, George	24	Farmer	Co Down
GAMBLE, James	25	Farmer	Donaghady, Co Tyrone
PATTERSON, Samuel	26	Labourer	Donaghady, Co Tyrone
WATSON, George	29	Labourer	Donaghady, Co Tyrone
SANDERSON, William	35	Labourer	Langfield, Co Tyrone
SANDERSON, Margaret	18	Spinster	Langfield, Co Tyrone
SANDERSON, Sidney	28	Farmer	Langfield, Co Tyrone
DAVITT, James	24	Farmer	Astraw, Co Tyrone
McGAWLY, Patrick	26	Labourer	Urney, Co Tyrone
GINN, John	28	Labourer	Drumceeran, Co Tyrone
GINN, Margaret	26	Spinster	Drumceeran, Co Tyrone
GINN, Jane	20	Spinster	Drumceeran, Co Tyrone
GINN, Anne	50	Spinster	Drumceeran, Co Tyrone
GIBSON, Mathew	38	Farmer	Drumceeran, Co Tyrone
GIBSON, Eliza	28	Spinster	Drumceeran, Co Tyrone
GIBSON, Fanny	18	Spinster	Drumceeran, Co Tyrone
JOHNSTON, Charles	38	Labourer	County Fermanagh
JOHNSTON, Ann	26	Spinster	County Fermanagh
KEYS, Thomas	24	Farmer	Magheramny, Co Fermanagh
KEYS, Eliza	20	Spinster	Magheramny, Co Fermanagh
CROW, Francis	22	Labourer	Magheramny, Co Fermanagh
GUTHRIE, Richard	30	Labourer	Magheramny, Co Fermanagh
CROZIER, James	20	Labourer	Fermanagh
CROZIER, Robert	22	Labourer	Parish of Dromash
BRISLAND, James	26	Farmer	County Tyrone
WOODS, Margaret	28	Spinster	Lissenderry Parish

| SHIP: | CERES | TO: | New York |
| SAIL DATE: | 5 June 1804 | FROM: | Newry |

NAME	AGE	OCCUPATION	RESIDENCE
TRONSON, Robert	17	Gentleman	Newtown Hamilton
HANLON, Thomas	26	Farmer	Armagh
HANLON, Judith	26		Armagh
LOVE, Joseph	23	Labourer	Armagh
LOVE, Rose	18		Armagh
PEEBLES, John	43	Gentleman	Hamiltonsbawn
PEEBLES, Ann	37		Hamiltonsbawn
PEEBLES, Margaret	14		Hamiltonsbawn
PEEBLES, William	12		Hamiltonsbawn
PEEBLES, Sarah	9		Hamiltonsbawn
PEEBLES, Annabella	5		Hamiltonsbawn
PEEBLES, Mary Jane		Infant	Hamiltonsbawn
MURRY, Ann	26		Fivemiletown
MURRY, Betsy	23		Fivemiletown
PATTERSON, Mary	34		Lisdromore
McCONNELL, Patt	24	Labourer	Moy
McCONNELL, Ketty	22		Moy
FORRESTER, Herbert		Master	
WYLIE, Alexander		Mate	
HARTFIELD, James		Mariner	
HAMILTON, William		Mariner	
YOUNG, Benjamin		Mariner	
DELENO, John		Mariner	
BLAIR, John		Cook	

SHIP:	LIVE OAK		TO:	New York
SAIL DATE:	5 June 1804		FROM:	Londonderry

NAME	AGE	OCCUPATION	RESIDENCE
UPDIKE, Daniel	32	Seaman 1st Mate	
MILES, John	39	Seaman 2nd Mate	
FLEURY, Samuel	20	Seaman	
GEERN, Fleury	27	Seaman	
McNAITH, James	27	Seaman	
GORMERS, John	24	Seaman	
CLINTON, Charles P	25	Seaman	
COLEMAN, Jonothan	19	Seaman	
ARMSTRONG, James	29	Seaman	
BELL, Samuel	25	Seaman	
BROWN, John	33	Cook	
WILSON, Henry	24	Farmer	Dungannon
WILSON, Jane	20	Wife to above	Dungannon
WILSON, Mary	2mt	Child	Dungannon
McQUILLAN, Mark	21	Farmer	Aughnacloy
PEDIN, William	22	Labourer	Aughadown, Co Derry
DAVIDSON, William	20	Labourer	Aughnacloy
GREER, Susan	40	Married	Cookstown
GREER, Sarah	20	Spinster	Cookstown
GREER, Susan	18	Spinster	Cookstown
GREER, Mary	14	Spinster	Cookstown
GREER, Hannah	12	Spinster	Cookstown
GREER, Anna	7	Spinster	Cookstown
GREER, Joseph	4	Child	Cookstown
DOUGAL, Sarah	20	Servant Girl	Cookstown
WEBB, John	50	Farmer	Cookstown
WEBB, John	19	Farmer	Cookstown
WEBB, Susan	16	Spinster	Cookstown
WEBB, Jane	44	Married	Cookstown
WEBB, Thomas	15	Farmer	Cookstown
WEBB, Maria	10	Spinster	Cookstown
WEBB, Jane	5	Spinster	Cookstown
WEBB, Alas	8	Spinster	Cookstown
HANNAH, William	22	Labourer	Armagh
HANAH, John	20	Labourer	Newtown Stewart
PATRICK, William	19	Farmer	Newtown Stewart
STEEL, Samuel	16	Farmer	Newtown Stewart
PATRICK, Jane	18	Spinster	Newtown Stewart
PATRICK, Nancy	4mt	Child	Newtown Stewart
McKEEVER, Alexander	21	Labourer	Gortin, Newtown Stewart
ANDERSON, David	20	Labourer	Gortin, Newtown Stewart
IRVINE, Alexander	21	Labourer	Gortin, Newtown Stewart
RUSSELL, James	22	Labourer	Dunnamany
RUSSELL, Elizabeth	22	Married	Dunnamany
RUSSELL, Isabella	5mt	Child	Dunnamany
SANDS, James	26	Labourer	
SANDS, Mary	26	Married	
SANDS, Robert	7	Child	Cranah, Moneymore
SANDS, John	5	Child	Cranah, Moneymore
SANDS, Ellen	1	Child	Cranah, Moneymore
SANDS, Mary	22	Spinster	
HUNTER, Joseph	45	Farmer	Gortimurry, Moneymore
McKEON, William	23	Farmer	Lisabany, Moneymore
McKEON, Ann	24	Spinster	Lisabany, Moneymore
BLAIR, William	20	Farmer	Newtown, Lemevady
MURDOCK, John	20	Farmer	Glass Lough, Monaghan
GALLAGHER, Patrick	21	Labourer	Furmeny, Omagh
GALLAGHER, John	22	Labourer	Furmeny, Omagh
McQUIN, John	15	Labourer	Cookstown
NcQUIN, Ann	17	Spinster	Cookstown

SHIP:	LIVE OAK		TO:	New York
SAIL DATE:	5 June 1804		FROM:	Londonderry

NAME	AGE	OCCUPATION	RESIDENCE
ALLEN, Osten	19	Farmer	Cookstown
CROOKS, James	60	Farmer	Cookstown
CROOKS, Jane	50	Married	Cookstown
CROOKS, Mary	20	Spinster	Cookstown
CROOKS, Margaret	18	Spinster	Cookstown
CROOKS, Samuel	17	Farmer	Cookstown
CROOKS, John	16	Farmer	Cookstown
CROOKS, Sarah	14	Spinster	Cookstown
CROOKS, James	12	Farmer	Cookstown
CROOKS, Benjamin	11	Farmer	Cookstown
CROOKS, James	6	Child	Cookstown
McKEON, Alexander	20	Labourer	Lisabany, Moneymore
McCUE, John	20	Labourer	Ternamenter, Co Tyrone
WALKER, James	54	Labourer	Dramagalagh, Co Tyrone
DICK, William	30	Labourer	Kilane Celperyt near Ballymena
GAULT, Samuel	30	Labourer	Kilane Celperyt near Ballymena
REED, Samuel	30	Farmer	Castledaunt near Newton Stewart
REED, Alexander	28	Farmer	Castledaunt near Newton Stewart
REED, William	23	Farmer	Castledaunt near Newton Stewart

| SHIP: | CATHERINE | TO: | Newcastle and Philadelphia |
| SAIL DATE: | 19 June 1804 | FROM: | Killybeggs |

NAME	AGE	OCCUPATION	RESIDENCE
CONYNGHAM, John	55	Farmer	Monargin, Killybegs, Donegal
CONYNGHAM, Isabella	49		Monargin, Killybegs, Donegal
CONYNGHAM, William	26	Labourer	Monargin, Killybegs, Donegal
CONYNGHAM, Isabella	23	Labourer	Monargin, Killybegs, Donegal
CONYNGHAM, Alexander	21	Labourer	Monargin, Killybegs, Donegal
CONYNGHAM, James	18	Labourer	Monargin, Killybegs, Donegal
CONYNGHAM, John	15	Labourer	Monargin, Killybegs, Donegal
CONYNGHAM, Catherine	12		Monargin, Killybegs, Donegal
CONYNGHAM, George	49	Schoolmaster	Monargin, Killybegs, Donegal
CONYNGHAM, Andrew	34	Farmer	Lochris, Mishue, Donegal
CONYNGHAM, Eliza	34		Lochris, Mishue, Donegal
CONYNGHAM, John	12		Lochris, Mishue, Donegal
CONYNGHAM, Andrew	6		Lochris, Mishue, Donegal
JOHNSTON, Robert	15		Donegal, Donegal
HENDERSON, Robert	45	Farmer	Lochris, Mishue, Donegal
HENDERSON, Elenor 1st	44		Lochris, Mishue, Donegal
HENDERSON, Elenor 2nd	19		Lochris, Mishue, Donegal
HENDERSON, Jane	15		Lochris, Mishue, Donegal
HENDERSON, Prudence	13		Lochris, Mishue, Donegal
HENDERSON, George	11	Farmer	Lochris, Mishue, Donegal
HENDERSON, Ann	8		Lochris, Mishue, Donegal
HENDERSON, Alexander	6		Lochris, Mishue, Donegal
FAWCET, Arthur	19	Labourer	Lochris, Mishue, Donegal
PORTER, John	43	Farmer	Lochris, Mishue, Donegal
PORTER, Eletia	44		Lochris, Mishue, Donegal
PORTER, Catherine	22		Lochris, Mishue, Donegal
PORTER, William	20	Labourer	Lochris, Mishue, Donegal
PORTER, Alexander	18	Labourer	Lochris, Mishue, Donegal
HARRAN, William	37	Farmer	Carrick East, Drumhome, Donegal
HARRAN, Elizabeth	37		Carrick East, Drumhome, Donegal
HARRAN, Ann	15		Carrick East, Drumhome, Donegal
HARRAN, Jane	13		Carrick East, Drumhome, Donegal
HARRAN, John	10		Carrick East, Drumhome, Donegal
HARRAN, Alexander	7	Farmer	Carrick East, Drumhome, Donegal
BROWN, Mathew	18	Labourer	Carrick East, Drumhome, Donegal
HARRAN, William	37	Farmer	Carrick Breeny, Drumhome, Donegal
HARRAN, Jane 1st	32		Carrick Breeny, Drumhome, Donegal
HARRAN, Barbara	11		Carrick Breeny, Drumhome, Donegal
HARRAN, Jane 2nd	8		Carrick Breeny, Drumhome, Donegal
GRIER, Thomas	30		Big Park, Drumhome, Donegal

SHIP:	CATHERINE	TO:	Newcastle and Philadelphia
SAIL DATE:	19 June 1804	FROM:	Killybeggs

NAME	AGE	OCCUPATION	RESIDENCE
GRIER, Jane	23		Big Park, Drumhome, Donegal
McCREA, John	24	Labourer	Lignanornan, Drumhome, Donegal
FAWCET, Catherine	21		Mt Charles, Inver, Donegal
DEVENNY, Elenor	27		Benro, Killartie, Donegal
SCOTT, Archibald	26	Farmer	Tullymore, Misheel, Donegal
SCOTT, Elenor	29		Tullymore, Misheel, Donegal
SCOTT, William	20	Labourer	Ardara, Killybegs, Donegal
McDADE, James	22	Labourer	Killarhel, Misheel, Donegal
LAMON, Andrew	18	Labourer	Adergat, Misheel, Donegal
KENNEDY, Patrick	52	Farmer	Meenhallw, Killymard, Donegal
KENNEDY, Susan	52		Meenhallw, Killymard, Donegal
KENNEDY, Edward	24		Meenhallw, Killymard, Donegal
KENNEDY, John	19	Labourer	Meenhallw, Killymard, Donegal
KENNEDY, Patrick	16	Labourer	Meenhallw, Killymard, Donegal
KENNEDY, James	13	Labourer	Meenhallw, Killymard, Donegal
KENNEDY, Charles	11		Meenhallw, Killymard, Donegal
McCAFFERTY, Biddy	20		Meenhallw, Killymard, Donegal
SHEERIN, Daniel	24		Ardara, Killybegs, Donegal
CARLAN, Michael	26		Killybegs, Donegal
MAXWELL, George	24		Raforty, Killartee, Donegal
LYONS, James	45	Farmer	Brackla, Killartee, Donegal
LYONS, Mary	40		Brackla, Killartee, Donegal
LYONS, Samuel	6		Brackla, Killartee, Donegal
LYONS, Elizabeth	4		Brackla, Killartee, Donegal
ALLIS, Sera	30		Drimahy, Done, Donegal
ALLIS, James	14	Labourer	Drimahy, Done, Donegal
McGLOGHLIN, Owen	29	Farmer	Glen, Donegal
McCLOGHLIN, Nelly	30		Glen, Donegal
McCLOGHLIN,	5		Glen, Donegal
GILLESPY, Patt	35		Glen, Donegal
GILLESPY, Peggy	24		Glen, Donegal
McCLOSKY, John	25	Labourer	Drimreny, Inver, Donegal
McCLOSKY, Rose	19		Drimreny, Inver, Donegal
LYONS, John	30		Glen, Donegal
LYONS, Catherine	26		Glen, Donegal

SHIP:	ATLANTIC		TO:	Boston
SAIL DATE:	28 June 1804		FROM:	Dublin

NAME	AGE	OCCUPATION	RESIDENCE
DAVIS, Sydenham	20	Farmer	Summerhill, Kilkenny
MORAN, Ralph	20	Labourer	Raheen, Kilkenny
RYAN, Michael	22	Labourer	Thomastown, Kilkenny
O'HARA, John	31	Labourer	Kilmurry, Kilkenny
HEFFERNAN, Hugh	22	Labourer	Clonsart, Kings County
MADIGAN, Walter	35	Labourer	Thomastown, Kilkenny
MADIGAN, Catherine	28	Wife to above	Thomastown, Kilkenny
SHORTELL, Andrew	21	Labourer	Thomastown, Kilkenny
NOWLAN, Daniel	21	Clerk	Tullow, Carlow
BOULGER, John	36	Labourer	Dublin, Dublin
BOULGER, Catherine	36	Wife to above	Dublin, Dublin
DUKE, Samuel	21	Labourer	Thomastown, Kilkenny
SWITZER, Martin	28	Labourer	Navan, Meath
SWITZER, Mary	28	Wife to above	Navan, Meath
MAXWELL, James	20	Labourer	Dublin, Dublin
GORMAN, William	32	Clerk	Dublin, Dublin
O,BRIEN, William	20	Clerk	Dublin, Dublin
KANE, Michael	25	Clerk	Dublin, Dublin
MALLON, Michael	33	Brewer	Dungannon, Tyrone
BOARDMAN, Henry	40	Lieut. Novascotia Infy.	
KEARNS, Anthony	23	Labourer	Dunleer, Louth
MELVIN, Andrew	25	Clerk	Bray, Wicklow
REYNOLDS, Thomas	22	Clerk	Keena, Longford

SHIP:	EAGLE	TO: New York
SAIL DATE:	7 August 1804	FROM: Belfast

NAME	AGE	OCCUPATION	RESIDENCE
BIGGEM, William		Farmer	Bushmills
BEGGS, Alexander	30	Farmer	Ballyroban
BEGGS, Margaret	30	Spinstress	Ballyroban
CLYDE, Thomas	21	Farmer	Ballyroban
McQUEON, William	39	Farmer	Bangor
McQUEON, Jane	36	Spinstress	Bangor
ROBINSON, Jane	28	Spinstress	Belfast
SEAWRIGHT, John	30	Farmer	Banbridge
SEAWRIGHT, Jane	30	Spinstress	Banbridge
HENRY, John	18	Farmer	Banbridge
ANDERSON, James	28	Farmer	Banbridge
NORRIS, Thomas	56	Farmer	Belfast
WARDEN, James	40	Labourer	Randalstown
McCRORY, Robert	30	Labourer	Randalstown
LIDDY, Hu	20	Labourer	Randalstown
BELL, David	47	Farmer	Banbridge
BELL, Patience	45	Spinstress	Banbridge
BELL, George	16		Banbridge
BELL, Thomas	14		Banbridge
ELLIS, Alexander	36	Farmer	Ballymena
ELLIS, Margaret	30	Spinstress	Ballymena
CROTHERS, John	44	Farmer	Randalstown
CROTHERS, Laifanny	32	Spinstress	Randalstown
CROTHERS, Jenny	68		Randalstown
ATCHISON, Nanny	21	Spinstress	Randalstown
WILSON, Jane	30	Spinstress	Randalstown
WARDEN, Joseph	26	Farmer	Randalstown
WARDEN, James	26	Farmer	Randalstown
CARROTHERS, Robert	35	Farmer	Randalstown
CARROTHERS, William	29	Farmer	Randalstown
CARROL, Elizabeth	22	Spinstress	Randalstown
YOUNG, Isaiah	28	Farmer	Monaghan
HOSE, Henry	25	Merchant	A Citizen of the USA

SHIP:	LADY WASHINGTON		TO:	Charleston
SAIL DATE:	21 August 1804		FROM:	Belfast

NAME	AGE	OCCUPATION	RESIDENCE
BOYD, William	57	Farmer	Dungannon
BOYD, Margaret	50	Wife to above	Dungannon
BOYD, Samuel	27	Labourer and son to above	Dungannon
SINCLAIRE, Robert	35	Labourer	Dungannon
WEIR, James	35	Farmer	Cookstown
WEIR, Mary	30	Wife to above	Cookstown
GOURLEY, William	24	Labourer	Cookstown
GOURLEY, Jane	26	Wife to above	Cookstown
ORR, Thomas	21	Clerk	Rich Hill
KENNEDY, Samuel	24	Farmer	Glenavy
IRVINE, John	44	Farmer	Loughgell
SLOAN, John	22	Farmer	Glynn
WILSON, David	30	Farmer	Loughgell
WILSON, Ann	27	Wife to above	Loughgell
WILSON, Margaret	60	Mother to David	Loughgell
COLVILLE, Joseph	26	Farmer	Loughgell
COLVILLE, Catherine	24	Wife to above	Loughgell
CRAWFORD, John	25	Farmer	Mounthill
CRAWFORD, Janet	21	Wife to above	Mounthill
AFTON, Alexander	25	Farmer	Mounthill

NAME	AGE	OCCUPATION	RESIDENCE
SUTHERLAND, David	33	1st Mate	America
NESBIT, Robert	19	2nd Mate	America
HARVEY, James	26	Seaman	America
FRONLER, Thomas	21	Seaman	America
GIFFORD, Andrew	22	Seaman	America
BARTON, William	36	Seaman	America
SMYTH, John	34	Seaman	America
BATES, Charles	19	Cook	America
ALBRIDGE, George	17	Boy	America
HEMPTON, James	13	Boy	America
DOUGHERTY, William	18	Boy	America
BRADLEY, Edward	24	Labourer	Letterkenny
WIER, Patrick	27	Labourer	Letterkenny
McLOUGHLIN, John	28	Farmer	Derryvain, Co Donegal
McLOUGHLIN, Elizabeth	28	Spinster	Derryvain, Co Donegal
McLOUGHLIN, William	5		Derryvain, Co Donegal
QUIN, Manus	21	Farmer	Drumran
CAMPBELL, John	24	Farmer	Muff
DEVENNY, Charles	21	Labourer	Letterkenny
PARK, William	20	Farmer	Coleraine
THOMPSON, James	25	Farmer	Castlefin
JERVIS, Thomas	30	Farmer	Pettigo
JERVIS, Sally	25	Spinster	Pettigo
McCONAGHY, John	25	Farmer	Pettigo
McCONAGHY, Jane	60	Spinster	Pettigo
ROSS, Daniel	25	Farmer	Magilligan
ALEXANDER, William	20	Farmer	Burt
McCARTER, John	30	Farmer	Bonymain
McCARTER, Rebecca	26	Spinster	Bonymain
DOUGHERTY, Joseph	30	Farmer	Muff, Co Donegal
DOUGHERTY, James	75	Farmer	Muff, Co Derry
DOUGHERTY, Elizabeth	58	Spinster	Muff, Co Derry
DOUGHERTY, Margaret	24	Spinster	Muff, Co Derry
TAYLOR, Ann	41	Spinster	Cookstown
TAYLOR, Walter James	14	Clerk	Cookstown
BLACK, John	30	Clerk	Cookstown
LEVERALL, Bernard	28	Farmer	Cookstown
ARMSTRONG, Thomas	21	Farmer	Enniskillen
THOMPSON, Hector	28	Farmer	Ballymoony
THOMPSON, Benjamin	26	Farmer	Ballymoony
THOMPSON, James	25	Farmer	Ballymoony
THOMPSON, Jane	21	Farmer	Ballymoony
THOMPSON, John	18	Farmer	Ballymoony
THOMPSON, Mary	15	Farmer	Ballymoony
THOMPSON, Elizabeth	12	Farmer	Ballymoony
THOMPSON, Rosan	10	Farmer	Ballymoony
McCAUSLAND, Conolly	22	Gentleman	Culmore
CONINGHAM, Henry	20	Farmer	Omagh

SHIP:	SUSAN	TO: New York
SAIL DATE:	5 September 1804	FROM: Dublin

NAME	AGE	OCCUPATION	RESIDENCE
McROBIN, Peter	22	Clerk	Dublin, Co Dublin
McROBIN, Jane	24	Married	Dublin, Co Dublin
MORRISS, Mary	22	Married	Dublin, Co Dublin
LAMBERT, Margaret	34	Spinster	Leixlip, Co Dublin
REDMOND, John	19	Farmer	Clossan, Co Wexford
WHELAN, Margaret	25	Married	Mt Rath, Queens Co
ROBERTS, James	22	Gentleman	America
MOORE, Henry G	20	Gentleman	America
MURPHY, Ann	25	Married	Dublin, Co Dublin
MORGAN, Alexander	38	Clerk	Dublin, Co Dublin
MORGAN, Elizabeth	35	Married	Dublin, Co Dublin
HIPWELL, Abraham	47	Labourer	Ballifin, Queens Co
HIPWELL, Ann	32	Married	Ballifin, Queens Co
SHIELDS, Henry	30	Servant	Poles, Co Meath
SHIELDS, Ann	27	Married	Poles, Co Meath
KERNAN, John	24	Labourer	Leahan, Co Longford
RIELLY, Bridget	30	Married	Belltrasne, Co Meath
KENNY, Mary	20	Spinster	Dunboyne, Co Meath
THOMPSON, George	29	Labourer	Queens County
WHITE, Christopher	30	Clerk	Dunboyne, Queens County
WHITE, Letty	30	Married	Dublin, Co Dublin
HUMPHRIES, ?	38	Gentleman	America
WHITE, Mary	18	Spinster	Dublin, Co Dublin
BENNES, Thomas	26	Clerk	Dublin, Co Dublin
ARMSTRONG, Archibald	23	Clerk	Killishandra, Co Cavan
ARMSTRONG, Jane	20	Married	Killishandra, Co Cavan
PHELAN, Patt	29	Farmer	Strabally, Queens County
PHELAN, Ann	25	Married	

| SHIP: | WILLIAM AND JANE | | | TO: | New York |
| SAIL DATE: | 18 September 1804 | | | FROM: | Belfast |

NAME	AGE	OCCUPATION	RESIDENCE
GARDNER, Thomas	35	Labourer	Belfast
GARDNER, Singleton	30	Labourer	Belfast
GARDNER, Alish	30		Belfast
GILLESPIE, Hugh	25	Farmer	Maherally Parish near Banbridge
GILLESPIE, Alexander	32	Farmer	Maherally Parish near Banbridge
GILLESPIE, Margaret	22		Maherally Parish near Banbridge
LOGAN, Hans	30	Book Keeper	Belfast formerly of London
McKNOWN, William	80	Farmer	Parish and town of Ardglass, Co Down
McKNOWN, Mary	67		Parish and town of Ardglass, Co Down
McKNOWN, John	32	Farmer	Parish and town of Ardglass, Co Down
McKNOWN, William	27	Farmer	Parish and town of Ardglass, Co Down
McKNOWN, Robert	19	Farmer	Parish and town of Ardglass, Co Down
WITHERSPOON, James	49	)Under bail to)transport himself	Knockbracken near Castlereagh, Co Down
WITHERSPOON, Margaret	48	)and sons to)America at the	Knockbracken near Castlereagh, Co Down
WITHERSPOON, John	21	)late Down Assizes)	Knockbracken near Castlereagh, Co Down
WITHERSPOON, James	14	))	Knockbracken near Castlereagh, Co Down
McCRUIN, James	31	Farmer	Tynan Parish near Keady, Co Armagh
McCRUIN, Sarah	26		Tynan Parish near Keady, Co Armagh
DENHAM, Revd Alexander	30		Town of Saintfield Co Down
DENHAM, Ann	26		Town of Saintfield Co Down
HUNTER, Joseph	22	Gentleman	Ballynur, Co Antrim
LIGGET, Alexander	22	Merchant	Templepatrick, Co Antrim
BLAIR, Margaret	19		Larne Town, Co Antrim
POOLE, J	30	Merchant	New York, America
McKAY, James	26	Farmer	Ahoghill near Ballymena, Co Antrim
McBRIDE, James	25	Farmer	Killileagh, Co Down
EARLEY, John	10		Ardglass, Co Down
WITHERSPOON, Eliza	10		Knockbracken, Co Down
WITHERSPOON, Henry	6		Knockbracken, Co Down
CONWAY, William	40	Farmer	Knockbracken, Co Down

SHIP:	MARIA	TO:	Boston
SAIL DATE:	18 September 1804	FROM:	Belfast

NAME	AGE	OCCUPATION	RESIDENCE
MITCHELL, Jane	40	Spinster	Magheragell Parish, Co Antrim
McMULLAN, Cornelius	64	Farmer	Loughinisland Parish, Co Down
McMULLAN, Eleanor	60	Spinster	Loughinisland Parish, Co Down
McMULLAN, Eliza	22	Spinster	Loughinisland Parish, Co Down
McNEIGHT, Robert	40	Farmer	Genavy Parish, Co Antrim
MONAGHAN, Edward	48	Labourer	Town of Monaghan, Co Monaghan
MONAGHAN, Bridget	18	Spinster	Town of Monaghan, Co Monaghan
HIGGINS, Michael	22	Labourer	Town of Monaghan, Co Monaghan
HIGGINS, Terence	20	Labourer	Town of Monaghan, Co Monaghan
MURPHY, Mary	24	Spinster	Lurgan, Co Armagh
WILEY, Joseph	28	Labourer	Donaghmore, Co Down
CONNILLY, Felix	22	Farmer	Mulloughmore, Co Monaghan
CONNILLY, Biddy	22	Spinster	Mulloughmore, Co Monaghan
McCARDELL, Pat	24	Labourer	Tetamel Parish, Co Monaghan
TRAINER, Thomas	58	Farmer	Tullylish, Co Down
TRAINER, Mary	58	Spinster	Tullylish, Co Down
TRAINER, James	20	Labourer	Tullylish, Co Down
McCLURG, Robert	22	Labourer	Magheradroll, Co Down
McCAMMON, James	25	Labourer	Ashaderg Parish, Co Down
McCAMMON, Rose	23	Spinster	Ashaderg Parish, Co Down
McADAM, George	30	Labourer	Ashaderg Parish, Co Down
McADAM, Elizabeth	23	Spinster	Ashaderg Parish, Co Down
McKEE, John	25	Labourer	Ashaderg Parish, Co Down
McKEE, Agness	25	Spinster	Ashaderg Parish, Co Down
DILLON, Arthur	46	Farmer	Crawford County, State of Pensylvania

NAME	AGE	OCCUPATION	RESIDENCE
McROBIN, Peter	22	Clerk	Dublin
McROBIN, Jane	24	Married	Dublin
MORRIS, Mary	22	Married	Dublin
LAMBERT, Margaret	34	Spinster	Leixlip, Co Dublin
REDMOND, John	19	Farmer	Clasan, Co Wexford
WHEALAN, Margaret	25	Married	Mountrath, Queens County
ROBERTS, James	22	Gentleman	America
HOSE, Henry G	20	Gentleman	America
MURPHY, Ann	25	Married	Dublin
HIPWELL, Abraham	47	Labourer	Balliper, Queens County
HIPWELL, Ann	32	Married	Balliper, Queens County
SHIELDS, Henry	30	Servant	Poles, Co Meath
SHIELDS, Ann	27	Married	Poles, Co Meath
KEIRNAN, John	24	Labourer	Leitrim, Co Longford
RIELY, Bridget	30	Married	
KENNY, Mary	20	Spinster	Dunboyne, Co Meath
THOMPSON, George	29	Labourer	Ballyhopan, Queens County
WHITE, Christopher	30	Clerk	Dublin
HUMPHRYES, Isaac	38	Gentleman	America
HUMPHRYES, Elizabeth	30	Married	America
BENNISS, Thomas	26	Clerk	Killishandra, Co Cavan
ARMSTRONG, Archibald	23	Clerk	Killishandra, Co Cavan
ARMSTRONG, Jane	20	Married	Killishandra, Co Cavan
PHEALAN, Patrick	29	Farmer	Strabally, Queens County
PHEALAN, Ann	26	Married	Strabally, Queens County
COALEMAN, Mrs	35	Married	Dublin, Co Dublin
SMITH, John	23	Clerk	Dublin, Co Dublin
SMITH, Martha	20	Married	Dublin, Co Dublin
PICKNALL, Hugh	23	Gentleman	Swords, Co Dublin
FITZSIMONS, Thomas	24	Farmer	Ballecondie, Co Cavan
JAMES, Susannah	17	Spinster	Ballybourgh, Co Cavan
JAMES, Thomas	12	Boy	Ballybourgh, Co Cavan

	SHIP:	DAVID AND GEORGE	TO:	New York
	SAIL DATE:	24 September 1804	FROM:	Dublin

NAME	AGE	OCCUPATION	RESIDENCE
BLUNT, Patrick	45	Labourer	Co Meath
SMITH, Benjamin	28	Labourer	Dublin
COSTELLO, Elenor	30	Servant	Dublin
SMITH, Edward	3	Child	Dublin
KAVENY, Patrick	40	Dealer in cattle	Sligo

SHIP:	CERES		TO:	New York
SAIL DATE:	19 October 1804		FROM:	Newry

NAME	AGE	OCCUPATION	RESIDENCE
ROATH, Roswell		Captain	
PORTER, John		Mate	
CLARK, John		Sailor	
HENDRICK, John		Sailor	
COOK, William		Sailor	
CADEVILLE, James		Sailor	
COOK, Thomas		Sailor	
CABBIN, Michael		Sailor	
DAVIDSON, Robert	50	Farmer	Rathfriland
DAVIDSON, James	52	Farmer	Rathfriland
DAVIDSON, Eliza	40	Spinster	Rathfriland
McFARLIN, John	38	Labourer	Rathfriland
DICKINSON, Gordon	38	Labourer	Rathfriland
TWEEDY, David	56	Farmer	Rathfriland
NUGIN, Rachel	40	Spinster	Rathfriland
DONNON, Joseph	29	Labourer	Rathfriland
DONNON, Jane	28	Spinster	Rathfriland
McLAIN, Hugh	21	Farmer	Sanfield
CARS, John	40	Farmer	Rathfriland
RYAN, James	30	Farmer	Banbridge
RYAN, Peter	25	Labourer	Banbridge
O'HEAR, Felix	40	Farmer	Banbridge
BYRNE, John	25	Labourer	Keady
BYRNE, Edward	27	Labourer	Keady
KEENAN, Patt	30	Farmer	Market Hill
KEENAN, Mary	24	Spinster	Market Hill

SHIP:	SUSAN		TO:	New York
SAIL DATE:	26 February 1805		FROM:	Dublin

NAME	AGE	OCCUPATION	RESIDENCE
FARRELL, Thomas	45	Labourer	Dublin City
ROCHE, Mary Ann	22	Married	Dublin City
DOYLE, Luke	22	Labourer	Dublin City
COONEY, John	26	Labourer	Dublin City
GRAY, Henry	24	Gentleman	Dublin City
HACKETT, Pat	26	Gentleman	Royal Oak, Co Carlow
FINN, Luke	25	Publican	Dublin City
KINSLEY, Michael	28	Shop keeper	Dublin City
BLACKAM, Henry	18	Labourer	Dublin City
BAIRD, Henry	36	Gentleman	Dublin City
BAIRD, Thomas James	9	Gentleman	Dublin City
CHAMBERS, John	25	Gentleman	New York, America
HUNDELL, Andrew	36	Gentleman	Delaware, America
MURRY, Patt	23	Labourer	Dublin
SMITH, Benjamin	30	Labourer	Kells, Co Meath
MONAGHAN, Thomas	30	Grasier	Granard, Co Longford
MONAGHAN, Richard	34	Grasier	Granard, Co Longford
RIGAN, Michael	28	Labourer	Granard, Co Longford
MOORE, James	24	Clerk	Dublin City
THOMPSON, Richard	21	Clerk	Dublin City
HACKET, Hugh	28	Clerk	Dublin City
KAVANAGH, Con	30	Clerk	Dublin City
KAVANAGH, Ann	28	Married	Dublin City
HAYES, Rachel	30	Married	Dublin City
HAYES, Andrew	7	Gentleman	Dublin City
WALKER, Abraham	35	Labourer	Dublin City
CRAWLY, Elin	20	Spinster	Dublin City
WALSH, Anthony	41	Sea Captain	New York
ROBERTS, William	48	American	New York
HYDE, Abraham	19	Clerk	Dublin City
FIELDING, Mary Ann	25	Spinster	Dublin City

NAME	AGE	OCCUPATION	RESIDENCE
MURPHY, John	35	Farmer	Welshtown
MURPHY, Mary	30		
NEILSON, Samuel	26	Farmer	Haydon
ALEXANDER, Richard	36	Clerk	Caloden
McCOLLUM, Angus	22	Clerk	Bangor
DONALDSON, Robert	22	Clerk	Downpatrick
REID, James	28	Farmer	Cockhill
TEIR, Thomas	28	Clerk	Downpatrick
GOODMAN, Miles	34	Farmer	Ballybay
PARK, Maxwell	50	Farmer	Larne
McCOMB, James	26	Clerk	Dromore
ANDERSON, David	40	Farmer	Portaferry
ANDERSON, Mary	40		
ANDERSON, William	14		
McMANNY, Samuel	28	Farmer	Armagh
RIDDLE, William	25	Farmer	Monaghan
FULTON, Thomas	20	Labourer	Ballycastle
CASSIDAY, Charles	23	Clerk	Belfast
ROBINSON, John	30	Farmer	Portavogey
McNEILL, Archibald	45	Farmer	Killileagh
McNEILL, Mary	40		
McNEILL, Thomas	17		
McCULLY, William	25	Farmer	Armagh
McCULLY, Robert	20	Farmer	
MARKS, John	24	Farmer	
DICK, James	23	Farmer	Gillhall
FERGUSON, Thomas	20	Clerk	Carmoney
BELL, William	28	Clerk	Lurgan
PARK, Mary	35		Larne
ORR, Robert	32	Farmer	Killileagh
McNEILL, Terence	15		
ANDERSON, Charles	12		Portaferry
BROWN, John	24	Farmer	Killead
THOMPSON, Adam	27	Farmer	
FULTON, James	30	Labourer	Antrim

SHIP:	FAME		TO: New York
SAIL DATE: 26 March 1805			FROM: Londonderry

NAME	AGE	OCCUPATION	RESIDENCE
DENISON, William	25	Mate	New York
NEIL, Isaac	32	Seaman	Pennsylvania
SMITH, Hugh	32	Seaman	New York
HARRIS, Robert	34	Stewart	Pennsylvania
BENAIRD, Paul	24	Cook	Africa
ROWE, Thomas	45	Seaman	Massachusetts
AUZBURN, John	20	Seaman	Maryland
ETHRIDGE, George	18	Apprentice	New York
DOUGHERTY, William	16	Apprentice	New York
HEMPTON, James	14	Apprentice	New York
HILTON, William	22	Seaman	New York
ROGERS, James	28	Doctor of Physick	America
ROGERS, Matilda	20	Spinster	Omagh
ROGERS, Alexander	17	Farmer	Omagh
ROGERS, John	15	Farmer	Maghera
COYLE, Hugh	21	Farmer	Garvaugh
GONELL, William	30	Farmer	Garvaugh
FREIL, Thomas	22	Farmer	Enniskillen
KERR, Mack	23	Farmer	Enniskillen
CALHONN, John	21	Farmer	Enniskillen
BUCHANAN, William	23	Farmer	Moneymore
BOTHWELL, John	26	Farmer	Moneymore
NETTERVILLE, Ann	42	Spinster	Monaghan
NETTERVILLE, Jane	12	Spinster	Monaghan
NETTERVILLE, Bess	11	Spinster	Monaghan
NETTERVILLE, Mary	9	Spinster	Monaghan
NETTERVILLE, Thomas	7	Boy	Monaghan
WHITELY, Jane	35	Spinster	Monaghan
McCLURE, Elen	30	Spinster	Monaghan
WRIGHT, David	19	Farmer	Castlefin
SCOTT, James	32	Farmer	Castlefin
SCOTT, Mary	22	Spinster	Rathmullan
KINKADE, William	28	Farmer	Strabane
KINKADE, Mary	28	Spinster	Gorten
COCKRAN, Hugh	56	Farmer	Gorten
JOHNSTON, Robert	21	Farmer	Rathmilton
HAMILTON, William	40	Farmer	Rathmilton
HAMILTON, Ann	38	Spinster	Buncrana
HAMILTON, John	9	Farmer	Cookstown
LOWREY, John	22	Farmer	Stewartstown
LOWREY, Elinor	24	Spinster	Stewartstown
CRAIG, Samuel	24	Farmer	Stewartstown
COCHRAN, Richard	17	Farmer	Tubbermore
ROGAN, Michael	22	Farmer	Pomeroy
KENEDY, George	50	Farmer	Garvagh
HAMILTON, James	19	Farmer	Garvagh
McCREA, Eliza	26	Spinster	Kilrea
BARR, Jane	24	Spinster	Ballymoney
McCLURE, Jane	50	Spinster	Ballymoney
HAUGHERTY, James	33	Farmer	Ballybofey
HAUGHERTY, Jane	25	Spinster	Ballybofey
HAMILTON, James	18	Farmer	Ballybofey
MOORE, Parker	20	Farmer	Buncrana
THOMPSON, John	21	Farmer	Rathmullan
SCOTT, Jane	20	Spinster	Rathmullan
SAMPSON, Rebecca	35	Spinster	Canican
SAMPSON, Sarah	30	Spinster	Canican
SCOTT, Daniel	54	Farmer	Donegal
DORMIN, James	47	Farmer	Donegal
McTULY, John	35	Farmer	Donegal
McTULY, Sarah	36	Spinster	Donegal

SHIP:	TWO FRIENDS		TO: New York
SAIL DATE: 1 April 1805			FROM: Belfast

NAME	AGE	OCCUPATION	RESIDENCE
MOORE, Joseph	30	Labourer	Drummara, Co Down
MOORE, Elizabeth	25	Wife to above	Drummara, Co Down
McADAM, George	27	Farmer	Drummara, Co Down
McADAM, Elijah	26	Wife to above	Drummara, Co Down
MURRAY, William	22	Farmer	Glessdrummond, Co Down
MURRAY, Thomas	25	Farmer	Glessdrummond, Co Down
AULD, William	21	Labourer	Aghaloe, Co Tyrone
WATSON, Hu	50	Farmer	Killcapell, Co Armagh
WATSON, Mary	50	Wife to above	Killcapell, Co Armagh
WATSON, Mary Jun	25	Spinster	Killcapell, Co Armagh
WATSON, Martha	23	Spinster	Killcapell, Co Armagh
DONAGHY, Edward	35	Labourer	Killcapell, Co Armagh
McMAHON, Alexander	30	Labourer	Killcapell, Co Armagh
McMAHON, Grizzy	27	Wife to above	Killcapell, Co Armagh
CARR, Joseph	20	Labourer	Killeleagh, Co Armagh
McKELVEY, John	21	Labourer	Ballycroon, Co Down
McKELVEY, James	30	Farmer	Derryneal, Co Down
McCAHERTY, Bernard	25	Labourer	Larne, Co Antrim
McCAHERTY, Mary	23	Wife to above	Larne, Co Antrim
HAVERON, Agnes	25	Spinster	Larne, Co Antrim
WILSON, Joseph	25	Labourer	Drummara, Co Down
WILSON, Mary	25	Wife to above	Drummara, Co Down
STRENAGHAN, Thomas	30	Labourer	Dehymeet, Co Down
STRENAGHAN, Elizabeth	30	Wife to above	Dehymeet, Co Down
ROGERS, James	50	Farmer	Carmoney, Co Antrim
ROGERS, Elizabeth	51	Wife to above	Carmoney, Co Antrim
ROGERS, William	16	Labourer	Carmoney, Co Antrim
ROGERS, Mary	16	Spinster	Carmoney, Co Antrim
WRIGHT, Jenny	21	Spinster	Bangor, Co Down

SAIL DATE: 1 April 1805   FROM: Dublin

NAME	AGE	OCCUPATION	RESIDENCE
POOLE, James	29	Gentleman	Dublin City
BRISCOE, Thomas	30	Gentleman	Dublin City
O'NEILL, Mary	30	Servant	Dublin City
O'NEILL, Catherine	7	Child	Dublin City
STITT, William	24	Gentleman	Antrim
ROBINSON, Neil	23	Gentleman	Dublin City
McDOUGALL, Dunkin	25	Gentleman	Dublin City
McGINN, Revd John	35		Dublin City

SHIP:	FRANCIS NIXON	TO:	New York
SAIL DATE:	16 April 1805	FROM:	Dublin

NAME	AGE	OCCUPATION	RESIDENCE
LEARY, Daniel Jun	22	Captain	New York
ATKINSON, John	45	Mate	New York
WALSH, Robert	30	2nd Mate	New York
HEANY, John	28	Seaman	New York
JOHNSTON, Christopher	24	Seaman	New York
KNAPP, John	27	Seaman	New York
MADDEN, James	20	Seaman	New York
WEAVER, Francis	22	Seaman	New York
THOMAS, Joseph	20	Seaman	New York
GIBSON, John	27	Farmer	Balyburne, Co Cavan
GIBSON, Elizabeth	22	Wife to above	Balyburne, Co Cavan
CAMPAIGN, John	20	Servant	Balyburne, Co Cavan
STEWART, Alexander	50	Farmer	Balyburne, Co Cavan
STEWART, James	18	Farmer	Balyburne, Co Cavan
STEWART, John	16	Farmer	Balyburne, Co Cavan
STEWART, William	14	Farmer	Balyburne, Co Cavan
STEWART, Alexander	8	Farmer	Balyburne, Co Cavan
STEWART, William	30	Farmer	Balyburne, Co Cavan
McGIBBIN, Stewart	22	Farmer	Balyburne, Co Cavan
STEWART, John	24	Farmer	Balyburne, Co Cavan
STEWART, Frances	45	Spinster	Balyburne, Co Cavan
STEWART, Agness	20	Spinster	Balyburne, Co Cavan
STEWART, Elizabeth	12	Spinster	Balyburne, Co Cavan
STEWART, Margret	10	Spinster	Balyburne, Co Cavan
STEWART, Jane	20	Spinster	Balyburne, Co Cavan
McCLAUGHNEY, Thomas	21	Farmer	County Longford
FOOT, John	20	Gentleman	County Cork
WILLIAMS, John	16	Gentleman	Dublin City
BEERES, Catherine	30	Spinster	Dublin City
BEERES, Mary	10	Spinster	Dublin City

SHIP:	QUANTIBAY COOKE		TO: New York
SAIL DATE: 16 April 1805			FROM: Sligo

NAME	AGE	OCCUPATION	RESIDENCE
FRANCIS, James	37	Labourer	Fartha
FRANCIS, Esther	44		Fartha
FRANCIS, John	16	Labourer	Fartha
FRANCIS, William	11	Labourer	Fartha
SMITH, Mary	20		Fartha
SHARPE, James	21	Clerk	Longford
SHARPE, Christian	24		Longford
GUNEGAL, Michael	28	Labourer	Magherow
GUNEGAL, Mary	26		Magherow
McGLOIN, Edward	30	Labourer	Ballyfarruan
CARROLL, Bridget	24		Strokestown
McGOWRAN, H	20		Boyle
McGOWAN, Michael	24	Labourer	Tyreragh
McGOWAN, Barney	26	Labourer	Tyreragh
MORRISON, Patt	23	Labourer	Tyreragh
McGOWAN, Patt	28	Labourer	Grange
HIGGINS, Patt	21	Labourer	Castlebar
McGOWAN, John	22	Labourer	Tyreragh
GILLESPIE, Neil	20	Labourer	Swineford
FERRELL, Catherine	23		Carney
FERRELL, Roger	26	Labourer	Carney
ROONEY, Laurence	21	Labourer	Jamestown
ROONEY, Nelly	20		Jamestown
EAKIN, John	24	Clerk	Jamestown
CLARK, John	21	Clerk	Jamestown
McGILL, James	28	Labourer	Sligo
McBRIDE, Patt	30	Labourer	Tyreragh
NEALES, James	24	Labourer	Tyreragh

SHIP:	BRUTUS			TO:	Philadelphia

SAIL DATE: 16 April 1805 FROM: Londonderry

NAME	AGE	OCCUPATION	RESIDENCE
BARCLAY, Samuel	25	Mate	Philadelphia
COLL, James	25	Seaman	New York
KAY, William	27	Seaman	New York
SHEDBURN, George	23	Seaman	New York
BOYSON, Peter	42	Seaman	New York
DYSART, James	21	Seaman	New York
BARTLEY, Robert	21	Seaman	New York
CHACE, Samuel	32	Seaman	New York
FARREN, William	23	Seaman	New York
MITCHELL, Alexander	31	Cook	New York
HOLLYWOOD, John	18	Apprentice	New York
FIFE, Thomas	14	Apprentice	New York
CRUMMER, John	20	Farmer	Enniskillen
ROBINSON, John	27	Farmer	Newtown Stewart
ROBINSON, Rebecca	27	Spinster	Newtown Stewart
CRAWFORD, Josias	27	Farmer	Newtown Stewart
IRVINE, Gerard	24	Farmer	Newtown Stewart
MARTIN, Charles	21	Labourer	Sligo
MURRAY, Francis	32	Labourer	Kilmacrennan
GORMAN, John	20	Labourer	Kilmacrennan
McMILLAN, Sarah	55	Spinster	Dungannon
McMILLAN, James	24	Farmer	Dungannon
McMILLAN, Robert	18	Farmer	Dungannon
McMILLAN, Sarah	15	Spinster	Dungannon
McMILLAN, Francis	12	Labourer	Dungannon
McKENNA, James	26	Labourer	Monaghan
KILLEN, Richard	20	Labourer	Monaghan
CHAMBERS, Alexander	62	Farmer	Ballymagrorty
CHAMBERS, Ann	60	Spinster	Ballymagrorty
CHAMBERS, Mary Ann	25	Spinster	Ballymagrorty
CHAMBERS, Sarah	28	Spinster	Ballymagrorty
CHAMBERS, Isabella	20	Spinster	Ballymagrorty
CHAMBERS, Rebecca	18	Spinster	Ballymagrorty
CAMPBELL, Arthur	22	Labourer	Ballymagrorty
SWEENEY, James	25	Labourer	Fannett
McCAFFERTY, William	22	Labourer	Strabane
BRIDEN, James	19	Labourer	Strabane
GREEN, Edward	42	Labourer	America say Philadelphia
FOE, Joseph	25	Labourer	Moville
STEIN, Thomas	25	Labourer	Moville
FOE, Barbara	35	Spinster	Moville
STEIN, Jane	30	Spinster	Moville
MARTIN, Alexander	23	Labourer	Moville
MARTIN, Mary	30	Spinster	Moville
ROGERS, William	15	Farmer	Omagh
BLACK, Margaret	25	Spinster	Omagh
McGILLY, Thomas	20	Labourer	Omagh
BELL, William	19	Labourer	Castledoay
DICK, Samuel	23	Labourer	Douglass
LITTLE, Thomas	18	Labourer	Douglass
WARDEN, James	40	Farmer	Randlestown
EDGAR, David	22	Farmer	Randlestown
McMULLEN, David	25	Farmer	Ballydonnelly
McMULLEN, George	16	Farmer	Ballydonnelly
GIDDIE, James	16	Farmer	Ballydonnelly
McMULLEN, Sarah	50	Spinster	Ballydonnelly
McMULLEN, Jane	22	Spinster	Ballydonnelly
McMULLEN, Mary	21	Spinster	Ballydonnelly
McMULLEN, Margaret	19	Spinster	Ballydonnelly
McMULLEN, Ann	13	Spinster	Ballydonnelly

SHIP:	BRUTUS	TO:	Philadelphia
SAIL DATE:	16 April 1805	FROM:	Londonderry

NAME	AGE	OCCUPATION	RESIDENCE
WATT, William	55	Farmer	Randlestown
WATT, Margaret	46	Spinster	Randlestown
WATT, William	24	Farmer	Randlestown
WATT, Thomas	16	Farmer	Randlestown
WATT, John Brown	13	Farmer	Randlestown
RIDDLE, Chr	19	Farmer	Newtown Stewart
HETHERINGTON, James	22	Farmer	Newtown Stewart
RUSSELL, Henry	16	Farmer	Newtown Stewart
CROSSAN, Patrick	23	Farmer	Douglass
TALLIN, Victor	21	Farmer	Douglass
LITTLE, Richard	19	Farmer	Douglass
McCROSSAN, James	18	Labourer	Cammus
SNEDGRASS, Mary	49	Spinster	Miltown
SNEDGRASS, Richard	23	Labourer	Miltown
SNEDGRASS, Elizabeth	19	Spinster	Miltown
SNEDGRASS, Mary	17	Spinster	Miltown
SNEDGRASS, John	15	Labourer	Miltown
LYNCH, William	25	Labourer	Tully
LYNCH, Ann	28	Spinster	Tully
LYNCH, Martha	23	Spinster	Tully
McMULLEN, Thomas	22	Labourer	Dungannon
McMULLEN, Sarah	23	Spinster	Dungannon
SMYTH, Robert	36	Farmer	Newtown Limavady
MITCHELL, John	22	Farmer	Ballymena
MATHEWS, Ann	50	Spinster	Movill
MATHEWS, Mary	20	Spinster	Movill
BARR, John	23	Farmer	Movill
PATERSON, William	22	Farmer	Movill
CLARK, George	30	Farmer	Movill
McLAUGHLIN, Elenor	29	Spinster	Movill
CLARK, Sally	26	Spinster	Culduff
McENTIRE, Robert	22	Farmer	Culduff
SMYTH, Robert	24	Farmer	Dunnamany
MACKLIN, William	17	Farmer	Dunnamany
CHAMBERS, William	23	Farmer	Coleraine
LAUGHLIN, Adam	25	Farmer	Coleraine
FORSTER, Mary	27	Spinster	Donegall
FERBERT, Rebecca	10	Spinster	Donegall

SHIP:	EXPERIMENT		TO:	New York
SAIL DATE:	25 April 1805		FROM:	Londonderry

NAME	AGE	OCCUPATION	RESIDENCE
EYKE, Jeff Tin	21	First Mate	New York
LOVE, Hugh	37	Second Mate	New York
BULLON, Jeremiah	18	Mariner	New York
SIMMONS, Edward	29	Mariner	New York
DAVID, William	22	Mariner	New York
WILEY, Reuben	18	Mariner	New York
ROBBINS, Thomas	20	Steward	New York
WILSON, William	24	Mariner	New York
GARDEN, William	21	Mariner	New York
CARTER, Cornelius	21	Mariner	New York
DYERMOND, William	26	Labourer	Stranorlar
HONE, Charles	24	Labourer	Stranorlar
PURVIS, James	42	Labourer	Cookstown
PURVIS, Jane	32	Spinster	Cookstown
FULTON, James	26	Labourer	Cookstown
FULTON, Mary	26	Spinster	Cookstown
ANDERSON, Alexander	30	Labourer	Cookstown
McCLOSKEY, Patt	30	Labourer	Cookstown
WHITE, Sam	19	Labourer	Ramelton
McLOUGHLIN, John	50	Labourer	Ballintoy
McLOUGHLIN, Martha	44	Spinster	Ballintoy
DOUGLASS, Ann	19	Spinster	Ballintoy
McCORMAC, Dan	20	Labourer	Ballintoy
DOHERTY, William	20	Labourer	Famell
KERNAN, John	25	Labourer	New York
MORROW, Henry	40	Labourer	New York
KERNAN, Francis	18	Labourer	Fermanagh
KERNAN, James	18	Labourer	Fermanagh
KERNAN, Manus	17	Labourer	Fermanagh
McMORROW, Henry	18	Labourer	Fermanagh
NORRIS, John	58	Labourer	Maghera
NORRIS, Martha	58	Spinster	Maghera
NORRIS, James	24	Labourer	Maghera
NORRIS, John	19	Labourer	Maghera
NORRIS, Mary	18	Spinster	Maghera
SMITH, Robert	25	Labourer	Derg
THOMPSON, William	25	Labourer	Killetre
McGRATH, Robert	23	Labourer	Derg
SMITH, Sarah	23	Spinster	Derg
SMITH, Margaret	23	Spinster	Derg
GRAY, William	29	Labourer	Donaghedy
GRAY, Edward	25	Labourer	Donaghedy
GRAY, Nancy	26	Spinster	Donaghedy
ROBINSON, James	20	Labourer	Donaghedy
GALLAGHER, Edward	25	Labourer	Fermanagh
GALLAGHER, Owen	22	Labourer	Fermanagh
CROSIER, James	52	Labourer	Tyrone
CROSIER, Mary	45	Spinster	Tyrone
McQUADE, James	28	Labourer	Tyrone
BEACON, Robert	40	Labourer	Tyrone
BACON, Catherine	22	Spinster	Tyrone
ELLIOTT, John	20	Labourer	Tyrone
ELLIOTT, Margaret	18	Spinster	Tyrone
BACON, Mary	36	Spinster	Tyrone
MOORE, John	36	Labourer	Tyrone
MAGUIRE, Patt	40	Labourer	Fermanagh
MAGUIRE, Bridget	30	Spinster	Fermanagh
DONACHY, James	50	Labourer	Fermanagh
DONACHY, Catherine	40	Spinster	Fermanagh

| SHIP: | EXPERIMENT | | | TO: | New York |
| SAIL DATE: | 25 April 1805 | | | FROM: | Londonderry |

NAME	AGE	OCCUPATION	RESIDENCE
MAGILL, John	19	Labourer	Ballycastle
KENNEDY, James	19	Labourer	Ballycastle
McREGAN, James	20	Labourer	Ballycastle
CAMPBELL, Andrew	45	Labourer	Badowney
CAMPBELL, Nancy	30	Spinster	Badowney
CAMPBELL, Mary	25	Spinster	Badowney
MOORE, Alexander	50	Labourer	Badowney
MARTIN, Robert	37	Labourer	Badowney
GRAHAM, James	26	Labourer	Badowney
MOORE, Isaac	29	Labourer	Badowney

| SHIP: | EAGLE | | TO: New York |
| SAIL DATE: | 25 April 1805 | | FROM: Londonderry |

NAME	AGE	OCCUPATION	RESIDENCE
THOMPSON, Charles	30	Captain	New York
CUMMING, William	30	Mate	New Hampshire
JOLLY, John	22	Seaman	New York
NESBIT, Robert	27	Seaman	New York
THOMPSON, Robert	48	Seaman	New York
DUNCAN, Robert	41	Seaman	New York
WYLIE, John	29	Seaman	Pennsylvania
HARDY, Benjamin	29	Seaman	Pennsylvania
LOIVAN, William	28	Seaman	Pennsylvania
WHITE, John	25	Seaman	New York
JACKSON, Moady - Negro	35	Cook	New York
FALKINER, John - Apprentice	16	But a boy	New York
DORRAN, Michael	50	Farmer	Rathmullan
McLOUGHLIN, Michael	50	Farmer	Buncrana
McLOUGHLIN, Mary	45		Buncrana
McLOUGHLIN, Ann	28		Buncrana
McLOUGHLIN, Hugh	27	Farmer	Buncrana
McLOUGHLIN, James	25	Farmer	Buncrana
McLOUGHLIN, Molly	20		Buncrana
GALLIER, William	28	Labourer	Banagher
GALLIER, Elizabeth	25		Banagher
GALLAGHER, Hugh	28	Farmer	Strabane
MULLAN, Michael	22	Labourer	Leek
PORTER, Samuel	22	Labourer	Leek
McKINLEY, John	40	Merchant	Antrim
McKINLEY, Marg	38		Antrim
HAGAN, Hugh	35	Farmer	Tyrone
WALKER, George	32	Farmer	Tyrone
McGRA, John	28	Farmer	Tyrone
McGRA, Nancy	30		Tyrone
CLARK, John	36	Farmer	County Derry
CLARK, Elinor	30		County Derry
LITTLE, James	44	Farmer	County Derry
LITTLE, Rebecca	39	Farmer	County Derry
GRIER, Joseph	21	Labourer	County Derry
McCARTHY, Thomas	26	Labourer	County Derry
FORSIGHT, James	26	Labourer	County Derry
WILSON, Thomas	30	Farmer	Donegal
WILSON, Margaret	28		Donegal
REILLY, William	27		Donegal
REILLY, Laura	28		Donegal
LYNN, Robert	28	Farmer	Leek
LYNN, Rebecca	30		Leek
LYTTLE, Eliza	24		Leek
LYTTLE, Peggy	22		Leek
PATTERSON, James	30	Labourer	Antrim
McCLANAGHAN, John	29	Labourer	Antrim
CRIMLISK, John	27		Antrim
CRIMLISK, Cath	27		Antrim
McMAST, James	30	Farmer	Ballymoney
GAMBLE, Edward	29	Farmer	Newry
McHENRY, Aran	41	Farmer	Newry
PORTER, James	39	Labourer	Boyleigh
CRAGMINS, Alexander	26	Farmer	Fintona
HUGHEY, Patrick	24	Farmer	Fintona
RAMSAY, William	24	Farmer	Fintona
CUTHBUTSON, James	24	Farmer	Fintona
CUTHBUTSON, Sam	18	Farmer	Fintona
GILLESPIE, James	26	Farmer	Fintona

| SHIP: | EAGLE | TO: | New York |
| SAIL DATE: 25 April 1805 | | FROM: | Londonderry |

NAME	AGE	OCCUPATION	RESIDENCE
BEATTY, Edward	28	Farmer	Fintona
ALLEN, William	28	Farmer	Fintona
JEBB, Rachel	30	Farmer	Fintona
GORDON, John	12	Servant	Fintona

SHIP:	DANUBE		TO:	New Bedford
SAIL DATE:	21 May 1805		FROM:	Newry

NAME	AGE	OCCUPATION	RESIDENCE
CLARK, James	30	Farmer	Coothill, Cavan
CLARK, Mary	31		Coothill, Cavan
STEWART, James	38	Farmer	Clonis, Monaghan
STEWART, Nancy	35		Clonis, Monaghan
STEWART, Betty	14		Clonis, Monaghan
McCLURE, John	49	Labourer	Ballybay, Cavan
McCLURE, Ann	45		Ballybay, Cavan
MOULAND, William	34	Farmer	Killishandra, Leitrim
MOULAND, Jane	26		Killishandra, Leitrim
MOULAND, Eliza	7		Killishandra, Leitrim
BOYDE, John	37	Labourer	Colvill, Monaghan
BOYDE, Eliza	32		Colvill, Monaghan
BOYDE, Molly	11		Colvill, Monaghan
ADDY, Thomas	42	Labourer	Lisarara, Monaghan
ADDY, Winpus	39		Lisarara, Monaghan
ADDY, James	7		Lisarara, Monaghan
CONOR, James	22	Labourer	Nabar, Cavan
STENNSON, William	27	Labourer	Butlers Bridge, Fermanagh
WALKER, Robert	39	Farmer	Balturbet
WALKER, Mary	31		Balturbet
McALDAY, James	27	Farmer	Killashandra
DRUMOND, William	21	Farmer	Killashandra
JONES, Sam	42	Farmer	Colvill, Monaghan
JONES, Eliza	47		Colvill, Monaghan
JONES, Kitty	4		Colvill, Monaghan
JONES, Mary	3		Colvill, Monaghan
CONAN, Peter	25	Farmer	Canygallan, Cavan
CONAN, Betty	23		Canygallan, Cavan
CONAN, Michael	3		Canygallan, Cavan
MONEYPENNY, Arthur	41	Farmer	Ballybay, Monaghan
MONEYPENNY, Eliza	40		Ballybay, Monaghan
MONEYPENNY, Kitty	7		Ballybay, Monaghan
THROUT, Will	24	Farmer	Killeshandra, Leitrim
McDONELL, Patt	31	Labourer	Killeshandra, Leitrim
BOYDE, Dan	30	Farmer	Killeshandra, Leitrim
BOYDE, James	38	Farmer	Colville, Monaghan
BOYDE, Kitty	37		Colville, Monaghan
BOYDE, Jane	11		Colville, Monaghan
BOYDE, Andrew	7		Colville, Monaghan
BOYDE, Thomas	6		Colville, Monaghan
HOWLAND, Gilbert		Master	
HOWLAND, John		Mate	
ODLE, John		Seaman	
LANDERS, John		Seaman	
BLAKE, John		Seaman	
CONGULL, Puro		Seaman	
ALMAY, Benjamin		Seaman	
NORMAN, Peter		Seaman	
JOHNSTON, David		Seaman	

SHIP:	ELIZA	TO:	Baltimore
SAIL DATE:	21 May 1805	FROM:	Londonderry

NAME	AGE	OCCUPATION	RESIDENCE
FOSTER, William	26	Mate	Massachusetts
SNODGRASS, Joseph	21	Seaman	Baltimore
SAUNDERSON, William	30	Seaman	Baltimore
REA, James	23	Seaman	Baltimore
OMALEY, Owen	22	Seaman	Baltimore
WARDEN, Rueben	22	Cook	Baltimore
JACK, Hugh	14	Apprentice	Baltimore
SHIRTUE, Michael	13	Apprentice	Baltimore
HESLIP, Joseph	11	Apprentice	Baltimore
FORBES, Joseph	29	Farmer	Omagh
FORBES, Ann	26	Spinster	Omagh
FORBES, John	21	Farmer	Omagh
KAIN, Robert	54	Farmer	Omagh
KAIN, Jane	40	Spinster	Omagh
KAIN, John	23	Farmer	Omagh
KAIN, Anthony	21		Omagh
KAIN, Elizabeth	19	Spinster	Omagh
RANKIN, James	34	Trader	America
RANKIN, David	44	Farmer	Bunison
RANKIN, Sally	50	Spinster	Bunison
RANKIN, Sarah	19	Spinster	Bunison
RANKIN, Elizabeth	9	Spinster	Bunison
OWENS, Thomas	30	Farmer	Dryn
OWENS, Margaret	30	Spinster	Dryn
HAYES, George	19	Farmer	Omagh
MOORE, Alexander	30	Farmer	Rossgull
GRIMES, James	16	Farmer	Rossgull
BRADLEY, Patrick	24	Farmer	Rossgull
BRADLEY, Catherine	20	Spinster	Rossgull
McCAUGH, William	25	Trader	Baltimore
McGARVEY, William	24	Trader	Baltimore
McGIN, William	44	Farmer	Clogher
McGIN, William	7	Boy	Clogher
McGIN, Eliza	32	Spinster	Clogher
McGIN, Samuel	5	Boy	Clogher
McGIN, Mary	3	Girl	Clogher
BELL, John	18	Farmer	Desartmartin
NIXON, Robert	19	Farmer	Killygordon
REA, Robert	18	Farmer	Killygordon
CAUTHERS, Hugh	28	Farmer	Aghanayran
CAUTHERS, Ellis	25	Farmer	Aghanayran
CAUTHERS, George	19	Farmer	Aghanayran
IRWINE, John	19	Farmer	Trisna
HENDERSON, Archibald	25	Farmer	Lowtherstown
HENDERSON, Elizabeth	21	Spinster	Lowtherstown
HENDERSON, Jane	4	Girl	Lowtherstown
HENDERSON, William	2	Boy	Lowtherstown
TAYLOR, Francis	18	Labourer	Fannett
JOHNSTON, Arthur	60	Farmer	Clooneagh
JOHNSTON, Catherine	55	Spinster	Clooneagh
JOHNSTON, Arthur	16	Labourer	Clooneagh
JOHNSTON, Margaret	18	Spinster	Clooneagh
JOHNSTON, Catherine	16	Spinster	Clooneagh
JOHNSTON, Jane	5	Spinster	Clooneagh
MULDUIN, William	30	Labourer	Carlave
MULDUIN, Mary	28	Spinster	Carlave
MULDUIN, James	7	Boy	Carlave
MULDUIN, Jane	5	Girl	Carlave
BARTON, John	35.	Farmer	Crugalughhill
BARTON, Mary	35	Spinster	Crugalughhill

SHIP:	ELIZA	TO:	Baltimore
SAIL DATE: 21 May 1805		FROM:	Londonderry

NAME	AGE	OCCUPATION	RESIDENCE
BARTON, Alexander	10	Boy	Crugalughill
BARTON, William	8	Boy	Crugalughill
BARTON, John	5	Boy	Crugalughill
BARTON, Sally	3	Girl	Crugalughill
McMURRAY, Patrick	24	Trader	America
WILSON, James	19	Farmer	Rusbay
PHILIPS, William	25	Farmer	Rusbay
ARMSTRONG, James	40	Farmer	Lasgaur
ARMSTRONG, Mary	36	Spinster	Lasgaur

NAME	AGE	OCCUPATION	RESIDENCE
SHIP: LEVINA			TO: New York
SAIL DATE: 21 May 1805			FROM: Newry

NAME	AGE	OCCUPATION	RESIDENCE
BROWN, Pearson		)	
LANE, Francis		)	
FREEMAN, William		)	
HUGHEY, Robert		)	
HARRIMAN, Alexander		)	
HYNES, James		) Master and Crew	
STEWART, Thomas		)	
DOSHMAY, Pear		)	
JONES, Asa		)	
STUART, James	30	Farmer	Cavan
STUART, Margaret (Wife)	40		Cavan
STEWART, Samuel	23	Farmer	Cavan
STEWART, Letitia (Wife)	20		Cavan
DONALDSON, James	24	Labourer	Cavan
DONALDSON, Elizabeth (Mother)	55	Widow	Cavan
RITCHEY, William	50	Labourer	Cavan
RITCHEY, Margaret (Wife)	45		Cavan
STUART, John	40	Farmer	Cavan
STEWART, Sarah (Wife)	40		Cavan
GIBSON, Samuel	50	Farmer	Cavan
GIBSON, Francis (Wife)	50		Cavan
GIBSON, Frances (Daughter)	2	Spinster	Cavan
STUART, Adam	40	Farmer	Cavan
STUART, Elizabeth (Wife)	40		Cavan
EDMINSTON, William	48	Farmer	Cavan
EDMINSTON, Margaret (Wife)	27		Cavan
TAYLOR, Thomas	50	Farmer	Cavan
TAYLOR, Jane (Wife)	50		Cavan
SILVIE, James	50	Farmer	Cavan
SILVIE, Sarah (Wife)	40		Cavan
SMITH, Edward	54	Farmer	Armagh
SMITH, Mary Ann (Daughter)	16		Armagh
CROZIER, Agnes	26		Armagh
CROZIER, Livy (Daughter)	2 mts		Armagh

SHIP:	EDWARD	TO:	Newcastle and Philadelphia
SAIL DATE:	21 May 1805	FROM:	Warrenpoint

NAME	AGE	OCCUPATION	RESIDENCE
ARMSTRONG, Jasper	37	Gentleman	Enniskillen
ARMSTRONG, Hannah	37	Wife to above	Enniskillen
PERRY, John	38	Farmer	Armagh
PERRY, Samuel	6	Son to above	Armagh
STRAIN, William	45	Farmer	Near Armagh
STRAIN, Mary	38	Wife to above	Near Armagh
STRAIN, John	16	Child	Near Armagh
STRAIN, James	14	Child	Near Armagh
STRAIN, William	12	Child	Near Armagh
STRAIN, Jane	10	Child	Near Armagh
STRAIN, Hugh	7	Child	Near Armagh
MAXWELL, John	17	Servant	Near Armagh
FULLERTON, Agnes	30	Servant	Near Armagh
RUSSELL, William	43	Farmer	Moneymore, Derry
RUSSELL, Jane	36	Wife to above	Moneymore, Derry
RUSSELL, Robert	11	Child	Moneymore, Derry
RUSSELL, James	8	Child	Moneymore, Derry
McBRIDE, Mary	17	Servant	Moneymore, Derry
MORROW, Andrew	26	Farmer	Newton and Down
MORROW, Agnes	24	Wife to above	Newton and Down
MORRIS, Ann	21	Spinster	Newton and Down
KELLY, William	25	Farmer	Rathfryland
KELLY, Jane	24	Wife to Wm Kelly	Rathfryland
KELLY, Ann	6	Child	Rathfryland
MINNIS, David	23	Farmer	Rathfryland
PORTER, Vere	40	Farmer	Rathfryland
PORTER, Elinor	30	Wife to above	Rathfryland
PORTER, Margaret	8	Child	Rathfryland
WORKMAN, Robert	40	Gentleman	Lisburn, Antrim
WORKMAN, James	40	Surgeon	Lisburn, Antrim
WORKMAN, Samuel	18	Gentleman	Lisburn, Antrim
WORKMAN, George	17	Gentleman	Lisburn, Antrim
WORKMAN, Jane	14	Spinster	Lisburn, Antrim
WORKMAN, Margaret	16	Spinster	Lisburn, Antrim
WORKMAN, William	12	Child	Lisburn, Antrim
WORKMAN, Agnus	13	Child	Lisburn, Antrim
ALEXANDER, John	30	Farmer	Ballynahinch, Down
ALEXANDER, Margaret	28	Wife to above	Ballynahinch, Down
SHAW, James	18	Farmer	Clough, Down
McGOWAN, Peter	22	Labourer	Clough, Down
BIGAN, Mores	28	Farmer	Rathfryland, Down
WRIGHT, James	26	Farmer	Rathfryland, Down
CROTHERS, George	21	Labourer	Rathfryland, Down
SHALES, William	26	Labourer	Dundalk, Louth
SHALES, Mary	26	Wife to above	Dundalk, Louth
GAMBLE, Robert	30	Labourer	Dundalk, Louth
MURDOCK, Sarah	45	Wife to above	Ahadign, Down
MURDOCK, Alexander	26	Farmer	Ahadign, Down
MURDOCK, John	20	Farmer	Ahadign, Down
MURDOCK, Samuel	26	Labourer	Ahadign, Down
MURDOCK, Robert	20		Ahadign, Down
MURDOCK, Margaret	10		Ahadign, Down
MURDOCK, Thomas	8		Ahadign, Louth
MURDOCK, James	6		Ahadign, Louth
MURDOCK, Sarah	20	Spinster	Ahadign, Louth
NEILSON, Hall	17	Gentleman	Ahadign, Louth
MOYNAN, Owen	28	Labourer	Co Tyrone
HUGHES, Andrew	35	Labourer	Co Tyrone
HUGHES, Jane	30	Wife to above	Co Tyrone
McCABE, Edward	35	Labourer	Mourene, Down
McQUOIN, Owen	26	Labourer	Mourene, Down
QUIN, Terence	40	Labourer	Mourene, Down

SHIP:	EDWARD		TO:	Newcastle and Philadelphia
SAIL DATE:	21 May 1805		FROM:	Warrenpoint

NAME	AGE	OCCUPATION	RESIDENCE
BYRNES, Matthew	26	Labourer	Newry
WILSON, Robert	28	Labourer	Newry
JORDAN, John	40	Labourer	Newry
McCOMB, Thomas	30	Labourer	Lurgan
RONEY, Daniel	24	Labourer	Loughbrickland
ANDREWS, Samuel	30	Labourer	Loughbrickland
GRAY, Francis	26	Master	Philadelphia
PLUMBER, Moses	22	Mate	Masachas
REYSDOCK, John	20	Seaman	New York
SHILCOT, David	29	Seaman	New York
MOORE, Robert	21	Seaman	New York
McDONALD, John	27	Seaman	Pensylvania
GIBSON, William	24	Seaman	New York
PETTER, Richard	24	Seaman	Pensylvania
LOWREY, Robert	19	Seaman	Pensylvania
JONES, George	22	Cook	Maryland
SMITH, John	23	Seaman	New York

SHIP:	LYDIA		TO: Philadelphia
SAIL DATE: 21 May 1805			FROM: Newry

NAME	AGE	OCCUPATION	RESIDENCE
REILLY, Francis	35	Farmer	County Cavan
REILLY, Mary	38	Spinster	County Cavan
REILLY, Catherine	8	Child	County Cavan
REILLY, Patrick	6	Child	County Cavan
HUCHESON, Jermiah	38	Farmer	County Cavan
HUCHESON, Darius	30	Spinster	County Cavan
McENTIRE, John	25	Labourer	County Cavan
McENTIRE, Mary	20	Spinster	County Cavan
CORRY, Nicholas	25	Farmer	County Down
BROWN, Nancy	24	Spinster	County Down
CONOLLY, Owen	23	Labourer	County Monaghan
STUART, Sarah Ann	32	Spinster	County Fermanagh
STUART, Elizabeth	26	Spinster	County Fermanagh
JOHNSON, Robert	45	Farmer	County Armagh
JOHNSON, Mary	40	Spinster	County Armagh
LITTLE, William	60	Farmer	County Armagh
LITTLE, Ann	55	Spinster	County Armagh
LITTLE, Sarah	25	Spinster	County Armagh
LITTLE, Jane	22	Spinster	County Armagh
POLLOCK, James	36	Labourer	County Armagh
POLLOCK, Jane	30	Spinster	County Armagh
PAUL, Samuel	29	Farmer	County Armagh
PAUL, Ann	25	Spinster	County Armagh
RAY, William	28	Farmer	County Armagh
RAY, Mary	24	Spinster	
MATHWLAR, George	36	Gentleman	Pensylvania, America
POTTS, William	24	Farmer	County Down
POTTS, Hans	22	Farmer	County Down
POTTS, David	19	Farmer	County Down
MURRAY, George	18	Farmer	County Down
BOYLE, James	35	Labourer	County Down
McKEADY, David	13	None	County Down
SMITH, Nancy	18	Spinster	County Down
WEBB, Thomas	44	Master	Philadelphia
STONEMAN, Samuel	42	Mariner	Philadelphia
MARSHALL, Abraham	35	Mariner	Delaware
WIDGER, John	25	Mariner	Pensylvania
GRIMES, George	24	Mariner	Pensylvania
VEXTRUIN, Samuel	30	Mariner	Pensylvania
BEAN, Joseph	36	Mariner	New York
ROE, Thomas	45	Mariner	New York
STRAW, James	15	Mariner	Pensylvania

| SHIP: | VENUS | | TO: | Boston |
| SAIL DATE: | 21 May 1805 | | FROM: | Newry |

NAME	AGE	OCCUPATION	RESIDENCE
MONTGOMERY, Will	56	Farmer	Killishandra, Co Cavan
MONTGOMERY, Mary	52		Killishandra, Co Cavan
MONTGOMERY, Jane	28		Killishandra, Co Cavan
MONTGOMERY, Margaret	20		Killishandra, Co Cavan
MONTGOMERY, Eliza	18		Killishandra, Co Cavan
MONTGOMERY, John	15		Killishandra, Co Cavan
MONTGOMERY, Henry	9		Killishandra, Co Cavan
MONTGOMERY, Jane	6		Killishandra, Co Cavan
SIMPSON, John	30	Labourer	Clonis, Co Monaghan
SIMPSON, Matt	30	Farmer	Belturbet, Co Cavan
SIMPSON, Robert	7		Belturbet, Co Cavan
SIMPSON, Mary Jane	5		Belturbet, Co Cavan
SIMPSON, Matt Jun	3		Belturbet, Co Cavan
KIRK, Robert	40	Farmer	Ballyhayes, Co Cavan
KIRK, John	10		Ballyhayes, Co Cavan
KIRK, Robert	7		Ballyhayes, Co Cavan
KIRK, Jane	5		Ballyhayes, Co Cavan
GLASEY, William	22	Labourer	Crosshill, Co Cavan
ATKINS, William	30	Labourer	Crosshill, Co Cavan
RICE, David	33	Labourer	Mt Gore, Leitrim
FITZSIMMONS, Peter	40	Farmer	Enniskee, Co Monaghan
RULPHER, Patt	30	Labourer	Redhill, Co Cavan
DIFFIN, George	25	Labourer	Coothill, Co Cavan
GOODWIN, Randolph		Master	
ADAMS, Dan		Mate	
CROWELL, Nicholas-Justin		Seaman	
NOLAN, Christopher		Seaman	
HARKINS, Thomas		Seaman	
RICE, Patt		Seaman	
GARDINER, John		Seaman	

SHIP:	POLLY	TO:	New York
SAIL DATE:	31 May 1805	FROM:	Newry

NAME	AGE	OCCUPATION	RESIDENCE
HICKS, Oliver		Master	
DUNN, Bernard		Mate	
HORAN, John		2nd Mate	
EMMETT, James		Sailor	
EMMETT, William		Sailor	
WILLIAMS, John		Sailor	
CLARK, John		Sailor	
CORK, John		Sailor	
SMITH, Arnold		Sailor	
SMITH, Archibald		Sailor	
BATTEIST, John		Cook	
STEWART, John		Cooks Mate	
PHILIPS, Grace	26	Spinster	
MURPHY, Mary	24		
CANON, Leslie	28	Gentleman	Ross, Co Down
CANON, Sarah	53		Ross, Co Down
CANON, Mary	26		Ross, Co Down
MONEYPENNY, William	29	Gentleman	Tandragee, Co Armagh
MONEYPENNY, N	24		Tandragee, Co Armagh
McCANN, John	50	Farmer	Tandragee, Co Armagh
McCANN, Judith	60		Tandragee, Co Armagh
MAGEE, John	28		Tandragee, Co Armagh
MAGEE, Bridget	28		Tandragee, Co Armagh
THORNBURRY, J	30	Farmer	Tandragee, Co Armagh
THRONBURRY, Mary	30		Tandragee, Co Armagh
McCANN, Mary	30		Tandragee, Co Armagh
FEGAN, Terence	21	Labourer	Ballymoney, Co Down
FEGAN, Margaret	19		Ballymoney, Co Down
McADOO, John	50	Farmer	Kiddavnat, Co Monaghan
McADOO, Mary	42		Kiddavnat, Co Monaghan
McADOO, James	20	Farmer	Kiddavnat, Co Monaghan
McADOO, Mary	16		Kiddavnat, Co Monaghan
McADOO, Jane	12		Kiddavnat, Co Monaghan
McADOO, Robert	14		Kiddavnat, Co Monaghan
ELLIOTT, Thomas	27	Farmer	Kiddavnat, Co Monaghan
KIRK, Jane	70		Kiddavnat, Co Monaghan
STORY, Andrew	31	Labourer	Kiddavnat, Co Monaghan
WHITE, John	48	Labourer	Balyborough, Co Cavan
WHITE, Jane	45		Balyborough, Co Cavan
WHITE, William	19	Labourer	Balyborough, Co Cavan
WHITE, Jane	14		Balyborough, Co Cavan
WHITE, James	12	Labourer	Balyborough, Co Cavan
CLARSON, Forbes	45	Farmer	Clenara, Queens County
DAVIDSON, Robert	48	Farmer	Rathfryland, Co Down
DAVIDSON, James	50	Farmer	Rathfryland, Co Down
DAVIDSON, Eliza	48		Rathfryland, Co Down
JOHNSTON, Robert	50	Farmer	Balliboo, Co Cavan
FERGUSON, James	28	Farmer	Drumlun, Co Cavan

SHIP:	ISABELLA			TO: New York
SAIL DATE:	7 June 1805			FROM: Newry

NAME	AGE	OCCUPATION	RESIDENCE
DORNAN, Margaret	62	Widow	Down
DORNAN, James	30	Farmer	Down
DORNAN, Jane	20	Spinster	Down
DORNAN, George	15	Farmer	Down
HUTCHESON, David	34	Farmer	Down
HUTCHESON, Nancy	30	Spinster	Down
HAMILTON, John	40	Farmer	Cavan
HAMILTON, Jane	40	Spinster	Cavan
COOKE, Francis	45	Farmer	Cavan
COOKE, Jane	45	Spinster	Cavan
COOKE, John	20	Farmer	Cavan
COOKE, Hu	16	Farmer	Cavan
COOKE, James	7	Farmer	Cavan
COOKE, Jos	5	Farmer	Cavan
BANNON, Patrick	35	Farmer	Down
BANNON, Ann	33	Spinster	Down
FARRELL, James	30	Farmer	Armagh
MOORE, Andrew	30	Farmer	Armagh
PEACOCK, James	27	Farmer	Newry
PEACOCK, Elizabeth	26	Spinster	Newry
DYSART, William	36	Farmer	Antrim
DYSART, Jane	35	Spinster	Antrim
BOYD, John	30	Farmer	Antrim
FOOKS, John	30	Farmer	Antrim
FOOKS, Ellen	30	Spinster	Antrim
McCULLAGH, William	24	Farmer	Down
McCULLAGH, Robert	36	Farmer	Down
THOMPSON, Robert	25	Farmer	Down
THOMPSON, Jane	26	Spinster	Down
THOMPSON, Mary	23	Spinster	Down
GORDON, George	25	Farmer	Armagh
HAMILTON, Alexander	50	Farmer	Cavan
HAMILTON, Elizabeth	50	Spinster	Cavan
HAMILTON, Mary	22	Spinster	Cavan
HAMILTON, James	20	Farmer	Cavan
HAMILTON, John	10	Farmer	Cavan
HAMILTON, Alexander	8	Farmer	Cavan
McMINN, Se	25	Farmer	Cavan
SMITH, William		Captain	
MICKAM, William		Mate	
PARRY, John		Seaman	
JARRETT, Jos		Seaman	
SMITH, James		Seaman	
JACKSON, Edward		Servant	
McEDORY, Patrick		Servant	
NELSON, Richard		Servant	
MASTERSON, Stephen		Servant	
FLOOD, Mathew		Servant	
ALCOCK, Jos		Carpenter	

SHIP:	SALLY		TO:	Philadelphia
SAIL DATE:	21 June 1805		FROM:	Londonderry

NAME	AGE	OCCUPATION	RESIDENCE
SAUNDERSON, James	31	First Mate	Philadelphia
CLEMENTS, Hugh	35	Second Mate	Philadelphia
BROOKS, James	26	Carpenter	Philadelphia
ANDREWS, John	21	Mariner	Philadelphia
ADAMS, Thomas	28	Mariner	Philadelphia
WILSON, John	24	Mariner	Philadelphia
DOLBY, William	40	Mariner	Philadelphia
WILLIAMS, John	32	Mariner	Philadelphia
KELER, Joseph	37	Mariner	Philadelphia
CALHOUN, Samuel	25	Farmer	Newtownstewart
DOGHERTY, Catherine	45	Spinster	Newtownstewart
DOGHERTY, Rose	14	Spinster	Newtownstewart
HARPER, Robert	46	Farmer	Lisnas Rea
HARPER, Isabella	40	Spinster	Lisnas Rea
HARPER, Jane	20	Spinster	Lisnas Rea
HARPER, Mary	18	Spinster	Lisnas Rea
HARPER, William	14	Farmer	Lisnas Rea
HARPER, James	12	Farmer	Lisnas Rea
HARPER, Christopher	10	Farmer	Lisnas Rea
HARPER, Robert	7	Farmer	Lisnas Rea
HARPER, Margaret	13	Spinster	Lisnas Rea
HARPER, Edward	5		Lisnas Rea
ARMSTRONG, F	50	Farmer	Rakeel
DOGHERTY, Edward	40	Farmer	Buncrana
DOGHERTY, William	43	Farmer	Buncrana
McCLEAN, Archibald	26	Farmer	Ballykelly
McCAFFRY, Bernard	24	Farmer	Enniskillen
KENNEDY, Henry	7	Farmer	Derry
STARR, James	23	Farmer	Fintona
STARR, Patrick	31	Farmer	Fintona
SMYTH, John	55	Farmer	Omagh
CAMPBELL, John	41	Farmer	Omagh
CAMPBELL, Ann	22	Spinster	Omagh
CAMPBELL, Elr	20	Spinster	Omagh
CAMPBELL, Sara	7	Spinster	Omagh
CAMPBELL, Alexander	4		Omagh
SMYTH, Mary	28	Spinster	Omagh
BARLOW, Agnes	35	Spinster	Lisdillen
McMULLEN, Robert	44	Farmer	Coleraine
McMULLEN, Martha	36	Spinster	Coleraine
McMULLEN, Margaret	16	Spinster	Coleraine
McMULLEN, John	10		Coleraine
McMULLEN, James	8		Coleraine
DERMOTT, William	27	Farmer	Ramelton
DERMOTT, Mary	30	Spinster	Ramelton
DERMOTT, Jane	27	Spinster	Ramelton
BAILLEY, James	50	Merchant	Magherafelt
BAILLEY, J	16		Magherafelt
MITCHELL, Joseph	35	Farmer	Clones
MITCHELL, Elizabeth	30	Spinster	Clones
HOPKINS, John	45	Farmer	Newtown Limavady
HOPKINS, Abraham	22	Farmer	Newtown Limavady
HOPKINS, Ann	24	Spinster	Newtown Limavady
HOPKINS, Jane	24	Spinster	Newtown Limavady
HOPKINS, Jenny	19	Spinster	Newtown Limavady
HOPKINS, Ruth	12	Spinster	Newtown Limavady
KERR, James	40	Farmer	Tyrone
KERR, Ann	38	Spinster	Tyrone
KERR, Elizabeth	20	Spinster	Tyrone

SHIP:	SALLY	TO:	Philadelphia
SAIL DATE:	21 June 1805	FROM:	Londonderry

NAME	AGE	OCCUPATION	RESIDENCE
KERR, Alexander	19	Farmer	Tyrone
KERR, Joseph	17	Farmer	Tyrone
KERR, Ann	15	Spinster	Tyrone
KERR, Jane	14	Spinster	Tyrone
ALEXANDER, William	17	House Servant	Tyrone
CRAWFORD, Robert	25	House Servant	Killeter
MAGUIRE, James	33	House Servant	Killeter
STEEL, Mary	45	Spinster	Derry
STEEL, Mary	20	Spinster	Derry
STEEL, Martha	18	Spinster	Derry
STEEL, Samuel	9		Derry
GILLESPY, Jane	18	Spinster	Derry
WASSON, William	25	Farmer	Donegal
FLEMING, William	23	Farmer	Tubbermore
LOVE, M	35	Spinster	Omagh
LOVE, Ann	9	Spinster	Omagh
LOVE, Mary	4		Omagh
CARSON, James	30	Farmer	Ballygawly
CONNINGHAM, Henry	22	Farmer	Omagh
HARDEN, Eleanor	14	Spinster	Dungiven

SHIP:	NANCY		TO:	New York
SAIL DATE:	16 July 1805		FROM:	Dublin

NAME	AGE	OCCUPATION	RESIDENCE
PORTER, William	15	Clerk	Irwin Street, Dublin,
FLATTERY, Pat	25	Farmer	Ballymahon, Longford
RYAN, Pat	22	Clerk	Dublin
DOYLE, Daniel	30	Clerk	Dublin
CAMPBELL, Thomas	18	Clerk	Drogheda, Louth
CONNOR, Mrs and her two children			Blackwater, Wexford
CHILD, Arthur	38	Captain	
McNAIR, John	28	Mate	
FAWCETT, James	19	Seaman	
FAWCETT, Thomas	22	Seaman	
CHILD, Samuel	16	Seaman	
HODGE, John	21	Seaman	
NICKLES, Samuel	18	Seaman	

SHIP:	AUGUSTA		TO: New York
SAIL DATE: 16 July 1805			FROM: Belfast

NAME	AGE	OCCUPATION	RESIDENCE
BISHOP, Samuel	22	Farmer	Killindry Parish, Co Down
LOURY, Edward	27	Farmer	Killindry Parish, Co Down
DAVISON, James	23	Labourer	Moneyrea Parish, Co Down
McCULLOGH, James	45	Labourer	Ballynine Parish, Co Antrim
ALLEN, John	21	Labourer	Gillinahisk Parish, Co Down
ALLEN, Thomas	18	Labourer	Gillinahisk Parish, Co Down
McWHINNY, John	22	Farmer	Saintfields, Co Down
CAMPBELL, Daniel	18	Farmer	Castlereagh, Co Down
FERGUSON, James	54	Farmer	Artray, Co Derry
FERGUSON, James	44	Farmer	Cookstown, Co Tyrone
CROYET, John	30	Farmer	Moneymore, Co Derry
CROYET, Wilson	20	Farmer	Moneymore, Co Derry
CROYET, James	18	Farmer	Moneymore, Co Derry
HARRIS, Samuel	16	Farmer	Moneymore, Co Derry
KILLEN, Jenkins	35	Farmer	Coorbilly, Co Down
McCARRY, John	54	Labourer	Ballycastle, Co Antrim
McCARRY, James	12	Labourer	Ballycastle, Co Antrim
CHAMBERS, James	22	Labourer	Drumbo, Co Down
WEIR, George	20	Farmer	Ballynure, Co Antrim
EAGLESON, William	40	Farmer	Killeads, Co Antrim
BROWN, William	12		Carmoney, Co Antrim
O'BRIEN, James	35	Farmer	Carmoney, Co Antrim
BAILIE, William	44	Merchant	Balfast, Co Antrim
PATTERSON, John	26	Labourer	Corncastle, Co Antrim
BEATTY, Richard	15		Hillsborough, Co Down
McWHINNEY, Isabella	60		Saintfields, Co Down
URE, Margaret	40		Drumbo, Co Down
URE, Jane	41		Drumbo, Co Down
URE, Margaret	15		Drumbo, Co Down
URE, Jane	13		Drumbo, Co Down
CROYET, Agnes	60		Moneymore, Co Derry
MARTIN, Margaret	24		Dromore, Co Down
EAGLEASON, Margaret	40		Killeads, Co Antrim
BROWN, Catherine	15		Carmoney, Co Antrim
BEATTY, Margaret	10		Hillsborough, Co Down

SHIP:	BELFAST		TO:	Newcastle and Philadelphia
SAIL DATE:	16 July 1805		FROM:	Londonderry

NAME	AGE	OCCUPATION	RESIDENCE
CANNAN, Geo W	25	Master	
RAWSON, Sheth	24	Mate	
SCOTT, John	20	Mate	
BROWNE, Geo	21	Sailor	
BONNOTH, Lewis	19	Sailor	
BURLING, Matt	24	Sailor	
DAVIS, Samuel	30	Sailor	
SMITH, William	18	Sailor	
COLES, William	28	Sailor	
BOYAN, Jacob	14	Sailor	
CALHOUN, Wm	30	Farmer	Claudy
CALHOUN, Jean	21	Spinster	Claudy
SMITH, Matt	22	Farmer	Claudy
DONOLY, James	45	Farmer	Six Mile Cross
DONOLY, Peter	22	Farmer	Six Mile Cross
DONOLY, John	23	Farmer	Six Mile Cross
DONOLY, Daniel	19	Farmer	Six Mile Cross
DONOLY, Patrick	17	Farmer	Six Mile Cross
RAFERTY, Wm	30	Farmer	Six Mile Cross
DONOLY, Margaret	45	Spinster	Six Mile Cross
DONOLY, Nelly	20	Spinster	Six Mile Cross
DONOLY, Susy	15	Spinster	Six Mile Cross
DONOLY, Peggy	10	Spinster	Six Mile Cross
DONOLY, Peggy	8	Spinster	Six Mile Cross
THOMPSON, Archibald	20	Farmer	Six Mile Cross
ARTHUR, Robert	24	Farmer	Omagh
THOMPSON, John	20	Farmer	Omagh
McCANNA, Patk	18	Farmer	Omagh
MITCHILL, John	24	Farmer	Omagh
FERGUSON, Andrew	19	Farmer	Omagh
RUSSELL, Isaac	21	Farmer	Omagh
GLEN, Wm	50	Farmer	Rockbrack
GLEN, Samuel	10	Farmer	Rockbrack
GLEN, Jean	53	Spinster	Rockbrack
GLEN, Margaret	20	Spinster	Rockbrack
GLEN, Jannet	15	Spinster	Rockbrack
GLEN, Jeany	12	Spinster	Rockbrack
KANE, Margaret	35	Spinster	Strabane
KANE, Isabella	14	Spinster	Strabane
KANE, Margaret	9	Spinster	Strabane
KANE, Will	21	Farmer	Strabane
KANE, Andrew	5	Farmer	Strabane
BENSON, Wm	25	Farmer	Strabane
MUNELL, John Sen	40	Farmer	N Limavady
NUMELL, John Jun	16	Farmer	N Limavady
SMYTH, James	25	Farmer	Derry
KELLY, Thomas	53	Farmer	Sligo
KELLY, James	35	Farmer	Sligo
KELLY, Wm	45	Farmer	Sligo
KELLY, Andrew	24	Farmer	Sligo
KELLY, John	14	Farmer	Sligo
KELLY, Jean	60	Spinster	Sligo
KELLY, Nancy	27	Spinster	Sligo
KELLY, Susy	20	Spinster	Sligo
KELLY, Elinor	18	Spinster	Sligo
KELLY, Elizabeth	14	Spinster	Sligo
WILLIAMS, Richard	38	Farmer	Strabane
WILLIAMS, John	22	Farmer	Strabane
WILLIAMS, William	14	Farmer	Strabane
WILLIAMS, Eliza	13	Spinster	Strabane

NAME	AGE	OCCUPATION	RESIDENCE
KELLY, Edward		Master	
FORREST, Geo		Mate	
PETERSON, Barnet		Carpenter	
TILLESON, James		Stewart	
WILSON, John		Sailor	
SMITH, William		Sailor	
DIXON, Robt		Sailor	
LAWSON, Peter		Sailor	
LEAVRY, James		Sailor	
SMITH, William		Sailor	
KENEDY, James		Sailor	
CONWALL, Amos		Sailor	
HERBERT, Anthony		Sailor	
CALLUSTER, Edward		Sailor	
CAFRIDAY, John	26	Farmer	Shamore, Co Meath
MURPHY, Pt	35	Farmer	Monaghan
MURPHY, Jane	9	Farmer	Monaghan
MOFFATT, Robt	25	Farmer	Killigarvan, Co Tyrone
MOFFATT, William	19	Farmer	Killigarvan, Co Tyrone
MOFFATT, Catherine	18	Farmer	Killigarvan, Co Tyrone
IRVINE, Wm	26	Farmer	Killigarvan, Co Tyrone
REID, Robt	35	Clergyman	Armagh
REID, John	$1\frac{1}{2}$		Armagh
REID, Jane	21		Armagh
STEPHENS, Mary	14		Armagh
JOHNSON, George	26	Farmer	Monaghan
STITT, Eliza	24		Monaghan
McCLILLAND, Wm	37		Keady, Co Armagh
McCLILLAND, Mary	40		Keady, Co Armagh
McCLILLAND, John	8		Keady, Co Armagh
McCLILLAND, Robt	6		Keady, Co Armagh
McCLILLAND, Jane	3		Keady, Co Armagh
BRAUNTIE, Richd	22		Keady, Co Armagh
MARSHALL, Betty	19		Keady, Co Armagh
McCEARIN, James	21	Labourer	Clontubrit, Co Monaghan
IRVINE, John	35	Labourer	Killmady, Co Monaghan
IRVINE, Margaret	23		Killmady, Co Monaghan
BEAUMONT, John	60	Bachelor	Rathfriland, Co Down
BEAUMONT, Andrew	17	Gentleman	Rathfriland, Co Down
BEAUMONT, James	15	Gentleman	Rathfriland, Co Down
DAVISON, Robert	50	Farmer	Rathfriland, Co Down
DAVISON, James	53	Farmer	Rathfriland, Co Down
DAVISON, Eliza	38		Rathfriland, Co Down
RENICK, Samuel	28	Merchant	Philadelphia, Penslylvania
CLASTON, James	18	Farmer	Monaghan
BARRET, Thomas	16	Farmer	Monaghan
HAIR, Anne	17		Monaghan
CROZIER, Wm	20	Farmer	Armagh
HARTAGE, Wm	28	Farmer	Aughmullan, Co Monaghan
HAWTHRON, George	22	Farmer	Aughding, Co Down
HAWTHRON, Mary	21		Aughding, Co Down
McCARNON, Thomas	26	Surgeon	Aughding, Co Down
BURGESS, Robert	20	Farmer	Aughding, Co Down
GALE, Henry	35	Merchant	Lisburne, Co Down
DUFFY, William	26	Farmer	Carrickogue, Co Monaghan
DUFFY, Mary	18		Carrickogue, Co Monaghan
DUFFY, Philip	21	Farmer	Carrickogue, Co Monaghan
DUFFY, Mary	17		Carrickogue, Co Monaghan

| SHIP: | ROE BUCK | | TO: | Philadelphia |
| SAIL DATE: | 26 July 1805 | | FROM: | Newry |

NAME	AGE	OCCUPATION	RESIDENCE
ANNOUR, Mary	45		Maragall, Co Antrim
ANNOUR, Eliza	15		Maragall, Co Antrim
ANNOUR, Marice	12		Maragall, Co Antrim
ANNOUR, William	12		Maragall, Co Antrim
ANNOUR, Samuel	5	Farmer	Maragall, Co Antrim
STEWART, James	50	Farmer	Gifford, Co Down
STEWART, Jane	45		Gifford, Co Down
STEWART, Alexr	23		Gifford, Co Down
STEWART, James	18		Gifford, Co Down
STEWART, Jane	10		Gifford, Co Down
STEWART, Sarah	8		Gifford, Co Down
STEWART, Eliza	5	Farmer	Gifford, Co Down
STEWART, Samuel	2		Gifford, Co Down
STEWART, George	1		Gifford, Co Down
MALCOMSON, James	23		Tanarague, Co Armagh
HANLON, Pat	36		Carrickmacross, Co Monaghan
HANLON, James	25	Labourer	Carrickmacross, Co Monaghan
REILLY, Edel	40	Labourer	Billurbert, Co Cavan
GRACY, Philip	28		Mountnorris, Co Armagh
GRACY, Jane	26		Mountnorris, Co Armagh
CARRAGHER, William	38		Castle Blaney, Co Monaghan
CARRAGHER, Peggy	40		Castle Blaney, Co Monaghan

SHIP:	AMERICAN			TO:	New York

SHIP: AMERICAN   TO: New York

SAIL DATE: 10 August 1805   FROM: Belfast

NAME	AGE	OCCUPATION	RESIDENCE
COLLINS, William	36	Farmer	Gilligan
HUME, Thomas	26	Farmer	Larne
REID, James C	21	Farmer	Hillsborough
McGLAREY, John	36	Farmer	Hillsborough
SCANDREL, James	30	Farmer	Hillsborough
McKEE, Robert	30	Farmer	Rathfriland
McMURRY, Hugh	28	Labourer	Randlestown
CAREW, Hugh	19	Farmer	Carncow
MARTIN, Moses	17	Farmer	Banbridge
McLAUGHLIN, Bernard	45	Farmer	Lisburn
BOWAN, James	24	Farmer	Saintfield
FORSYTHE, Thomas	18	Labourer	Clough
ADDISON, Thomas	27	Farmer	Carrickfergus
HADDOCK, James	66	Farmer	Armagh
DESERT, William	45	Farmer	Dromore
STEWART, Samuel	18	Clerk	Ballycastle
WHITE, William	24	Labourer	Belfast
HADDOCK, Henry	20	Farmer	Richhill
THOMPSON, James	20	Labourer	Craigs
SINCLAIR, John	23	Grocer	Kirkcubbin
RANKIN, John	30	Doctor	Kirkcubbin
CAMPBELL, Samuel	24	Farmer	Dromore
JOHNSTON, James	32	Labourer	Ahoghill
THOMPSON, Hugh	46	Farmer	Antrim
BELL, Robert	25	Farmer	Killileagh
FULTON, Thomas	31	Farmer	Killileagh
FERGUSON, Thomas	37	Farmer	Armagh
McCULLY, William	22	Farmer	Killiliagh
DICK, James	25	Labourer	Monaghan
RIDDALL, Hugh	28	Farmer	Crumlin
JAMESON, William	19	Clerk	Lisburn
GRAHAM, James	24	Labourer	Ballycastle
WALKER, Thomas	39	Farmer	Bangor
HULL, William	34	Farmer	Randlestown
SMART, John	28	Labourer	Armagh
BEARNS, Henry		Master	
McNATERY, George		Chief Mate	
CAMPBELL, Daniel		Second Mate	
KALDOR, Connell		Carpenter	
SANDERS, Joseph		Seaman	
WOOLDERRAY, John		Seaman	
THOP, Amos		Seaman	
THOMPSON, John		Seaman	
BROWN, William		Seaman	
HYAS, William		Steward	
HUDSON, Samuel		Cook	
CARLISLE, James		Apprentice	

SHIP:	DEMOSCOTTA		TO:	Boston
SAIL DATE:	30 August 1805		FROM:	Dublin

NAME	AGE	OCCUPATION	RESIDENCE
JAMESON, James	24	Labourer	Inistioge, Kilkenny
MICHAEL, Tony	23	Clerk	Inistioge, Kilkenny
WHELAN, Stephen	31	Clerk	Carrick on suir, Waterford
POWER, Mary			Inistioge, Kilkenny
KAVANAGH, Roy			Inistioge, Kilkenny
FOY, John		Seaman	American
CLOONEY, Michael		Seaman	American
BERRY, Edward		Seaman	American
MORGAN, John		Seaman	American
POWERS, James		Seaman	American
BROWNE, James		Seaman	American
COLE, Thomas		Seaman	American
YORK, Henry		Seaman	American

SHIP:	MARY		TO:	Charlestown South Carolina

SAIL DATE: 17 September 1805   FROM: Belfast

NAME	AGE	OCCUPATION	RESIDENCE
PARKS, James		Merchant	Belfast
SHANNON, John			Abbyville, S Carolina
IRVINE, Charles	65	Farmer	Loughgeel
IRVINE, Robert	40	Farmer	Loughgeel
LYNN, William	34	Farmer	Loughgeel
LYNN, Rebecca		Wife to above	Loughgeel
WILSON, John	34	Farmer	Kilmanda
WILSON, Jennett		Wife to above	Kilmanda
McHENRY, Daniel	50	Farmer	Callagan
McHENRY, Eleanor		Wife to above	Callagan
CUMMING, Jennett	25		Donegore
CUMMING, Eleanor	22		Donegore
HAGAN, Edward	60		Carrickfergus
HAGAN, Agnes		Wife to above	Carrickfergus
BURNS, Samuel	45	Farmer	Loughgeel
BURNS, Agnes	40	Wife to above	Loughgeel
GORDON, Thomas	30	Farmer	Mounthill
GORDON, Elizabeth	27	Wife to above	Mounthill
DICKEY, John	55	Carman	Ballymena
CLARKE, Sheather		Captain	
McTIER, Abraham		Mate	
WHITE, John			
PURCELL, John			
LARMORE, William			
CLARKE, Tobias			
BURTON, John			
DINNISON, Laurence			

```
SHIP:       PANDORA                                    TO:   New York
SAIL DATE:  17 September 1805                           FROM: Sligo
```

NAME	AGE	OCCUPATION	RESIDENCE
LANG, James	27	Master	
JOHNSON, Alexander	25	1st Mate	
BROWNE, Ralpf	29	2nd Mate	
McGRATLE, Denis	22	Mariner	
WILSON, John	22	Mariner	
CRAWFORD, William	26	Mariner	
ELLIOTT, Thomas	16	Mariner	
KERKLAW, John	23	Mariner	
CONNOR, John	21	Labourer	Enniskillen
COX, John	23	Labourer	Enniskillen
HORAN, Pat	19	Labourer	Ballymate
TIGHE, James	28	Labourer	Ballymate
McDONOUGHE, Pat	29	Labourer	Ballymate
GARRIGLE, Michael	30	Labourer	Tyeragh
McGOWEN, John	25	Labourer	Tyeragh
McMURRY, Darby	23	Labourer	Tyeragh
ROARKE, Patt	20	Labourer	Drumfrice
CARRAWAY, Thomas	19	Labourer	Drumfrice
McGOWAN, Bernard	13	Labourer	Downpatrick
RYAN, Thomas	40	Labourer	Ballyshannon
LYNCH, Andrew	34	Labourer	Tyreragh
EVERAID, ?	45	Labourer	Tyreragh
HARKIN, Peter	33	Labourer	Erris
HIGGINS, P	26	Labourer	Erris
WHITEINDALE, Robert	25	Clerk	Dublin
COCHRAN, John	26	Clerk	Dublin
MORAN, Thomas	21	Clerk	Sligo
IRVINE, Henry	18	Clerk	Sligo
O'BRIEN, Oliver	28	Labourer	Donegal
HENDERSON, Robert	21	Labourer	Barrow
BRENAN, Nathaniel	26	Labourer	Barrow
CONWAY, Andrew	29	Labourer	Barrow
CONWAY, Ann	28		Barrow
O'NEIL, Jane	30		Sligo
O'NEIL, Henry	10		Sligo
CLEARY, Judy	18	Servant	Sligo
CORTELLO, Mary	24		Ballyweeney
ANDERSON, Bill	20		Sligo
HARKIND, Catherine	28		Ballycarron
HARKIND, Bridget	21		Ballycarron
O'NEIL, Jane	12		Sligo
KEVENEY, Hannah	38		Sligo
KEVENEY, Margaret	17		Sligo
KEVENEY, William	14		Sligo
REDWARD, Bernard	48	Gentleman	Sligo
REDWARD, William	12	Gentleman	Sligo
REDWARD, Margaret	20	Gentleman	Sligo
REDWARD, Ann	21	Gentleman	Sligo
REDWARD, Atty	18		Sligo
REDWARD, Eliz	16		Sligo
REDWARD, Henry	6		Sligo
McDOWELL, Jane	32	Servant	Castlebar
O'BURNE, Jane	21	Servant	Castlebar
WHITE, Thomas	26	Servant	Castlebar
BURROWS, Thomas	29	Labourer	Erris
BURROWS, Ann	28		Erris
O'GARA, Andrew	36	Labourer	Ballinrobe
O'GARA, Mary	33		Ballinrobe
O'GARA, Henry	15	Labourer	Ballinrobe
O'GARA, Anna	10		Ballinrobe

SHIP:	PANDORA		TO:	New York
SAIL DATE: 17 September 1805			FROM:	Sligo

NAME	AGE	OCCUPATION	RESIDENCE
SWEENEY, Adam	20	Clerk	Grange
SWEENEY, Ann	18		Grange
HENDERSON, George	30	Clerk	Halfway House
HENDERSON, Mary	26		Halfway House
STEEL, Andrew	21	Schoolmaster	Ballisodane
STEEL, Mary	20		Ballisodane
STEEL, Henry	2		Ballisodane
GERAHTY, Martin	29	Labourer	Sligo
GERAHTY, Nancy	26		Sligo
PETERS, Andrew	23	Labourer	Ballynewry
PETERS, Mary	22		Ballynewry
CAULFIELD, Henry	26	Labourer	
CAULFIELD, Mathew	24	Labourer	
ARMSTRONG, John	22	Surgeon	Sligo
SWEENEY, Peter	19	Labourer	Grange

NAME	AGE	OCCUPATION	RESIDENCE
THOMPSON, Charles	34	Master	New York
CUMMING, William	31	Chief Mate	New York
BARTLEY, Robert	25	Boatswain	New York
PETTERS, Alex	25	Seaman	
FERRISS, Joseph	34	Seaman	
YOUNG, John	24	Seaman	
MITCHELL, John	26	Seaman	
McLAUGHLIN, James	22	Seaman	
RUDAY, Thomas	35	Seaman	
FALKNER, John	18	Apprentice	
KING, James	32	Cook	
HOMES, Charles	15	Boy	
HIGGINS, Francis	50	Gentleman	Philadelphia
CARR, Henry	26	Clerk	Dublin
COLGIN, Joseph	40	Porter	Dublin
COLGIN, Catherine	30	Wife to above	Dublin
COLGIN, Richard	8	Child	Dublin
COLGIN, Margaret	9	Child	Dublin
COLGIN, John	4	Child	Dublin
COLGIN, Terrence	2	Child	Dublin
PARROTT, John	40	Warehouse Clerk	Dublin
PARROTT, Judith	35	Wife to above	Dublin
PARROTT, Richard	12	Child	Dublin
PARROTT, John	10	Child	Dublin
PARROTT, William	8	Child	Dublin
PARROTT, Winfred	11	Child	Dublin
PARROTT, Catherine	11	Child	Dublin
PARROTT, Mary	6	Child	Dublin
BUTLER, Richard	21	Clerk	Dublin
COX, Thomas	19	Labourer	Lonford

SHIP:	GRACE		TO:	New York
SAIL DATE:	29 November 1805		FROM:	Belfast

NAME	AGE	OCCUPATION	RESIDENCE
McAULEY, Samuel	25	Student	Rathfryland, Co Down
CAULSON, John	21	Labourer	Loughbrickland, Co Down
DICK, William	25	Labourer	Drumarra, Co Down
DICK, Jane	25		Drumarra, Co Down
HAWLOR, Robert	28	Farmer	Killiman, Co Tyrone
McMULLEN, James	19	Labourer	Donaghmore, Co Down
HAMILTON, Robert	22	Farmer	Killiard, Co Antrim
REILLY, Marlow	48	Merchant	Carrickfergus, Co Antrim
KINSLEY, James	24	Farmer	Glenevy, Co Antrim
BAMBER, Robert	28	Labourer	Baughon, Co Down
MULLIGAN, Michael	40	Farmer	Cavan, Co Cavan
DAVIS, William	35	Musician	Belfast, Co Antrim
BAMBER, Margaret	25		Bangor, Co Down
JAMESON, David	45	Farmer	Braid, Co Antrim
BLACK, George	18	Labourer	Braid, Co Antrim
MULLIGAN, Alice	30		Cavan, Co Cavan
MATHEWS, Robert		Master of New York	
WALSH, Robert		First Mate	
JOHNSON, Christopher		Second Mate	
CARRELL, James		Cook	
KING, Robert		Steward	
ROBINSON, Charles		Seaman	
LYNCH, Martin		Seaman	
HATFIELD, James		Seaman	
WILKINSON, Henry		Seaman	
KIRK, William		Seaman	
RICHER, Robert		Seaman	
PLUMBER, Samuel		Seaman	

NAME	AGE	OCCUPATION	RESIDENCE
CROSS, Alex	24	Gentleman	Boyle
HOPKINS, Hannah	30	Merchant	Leith
SHARNAN, George	18	Gentleman	Dublin
ENGLISH, Edward	25	Labourer	Michalstown, Cork
CONNELL, Philip	30	Labourer	Kells, Meath
TOBIN, Edward	25	Labourer	Kells, Meath
NAK, John	17	Gentleman	Liverpool
BLACK, Thomas	17	Gentleman	
GARVEY, John	25		
GIBSON, Charles W	32	Gentleman	London
WILSON, Thomas	22	Farmer	Castle Polard, West Meath
CALBECK, Eaton	20	Clerk	Rath Danny, Queens County
FITZSIMMONS, William	21	Labourer	Downpatrick, Co Down
FITZSIMMONS, Richard	64	Labourer	Downpatrick, Co Down
FITZSIMMONS, Eliza	25	Spinster	Downpatrick, Co Down
FITZSIMMONS, Anne	18	Spinster	Downpatrick, Co Down
WEST, Louis	25	Clerk	Dublin
O'CONNOR, Michael	20	Clerk	Dublin
COLLINS, Mark		Master	American
ALLEN, Joseph		Mate	American
MOORE, John		Sailor	American
MOFFIN, John		Sailor	American
REILY, Philip		Sailor	American
ALLEN, James		Sailor	American
ALLEN, James		Sailor	American
BABTIST, John		Sailor	American
COLLINS, Mark Jun		Sailor	American
PINDERGAST, Michael		Sailor	American
VIVACIVA, Francis		Sailor	American

SHIP:	WILLIAM PENN		TO: New York
SAIL DATE:	25 February 1806		FROM: Newry

NAME	AGE	OCCUPATION	RESIDENCE
HUPEY, Barzilea		Master	
MANHALE, Thomas		Mate	
BLACK, William		Carpenter	
CHRISTAIN, Jacob		Seaman	
TINNET, John		Crew	
BRYAN, Martin		Crew	
CARROLL, Samuel		Crew	
RUCHARD, Richard		Crew	
FREEMAN, Nathan		Crew	
SHERMAN, George		Crew	
BADA, John		Crew	
CARROLL, John		Crew	
BROWN, John		Crew	
CONNOR, William		Crew	
JONES, John		Crew	
REID, Charles		Crew	
SMITH, James	26	Labourer	Castleblaney
MARTIN, William	30	Labourer	Carrickmacross
MARTIN, James	26	Spinster	Carrickmacross
MARTIN, Susan	6		Carrickmacross
MARTIN, Eliza	4		Carrickmacross
MARTIN, Mary	3		Carrickmacross
JOHNSTON, Thomas	26	Labourer	Dundalk
McDONALL, Alexander	31	Labourer	Dundalk
MOOREHEAD, James	36	Labourer	Monaghan
SMITH, Patrick	24	Labourer	Monaghan
MULLIN, William	30	Labourer	Armagh
MULLIN, James	26	Labourer	Armagh
MULLIN, Jane	24	Spinster	Armagh
MULLIN, Susan	12	Spinster	Armagh
McSHANE, Michael	25	Labourer	Armagh
RICE, Terence	28	Labourer	Pointspass
RICE, Eliza	22	Spinster	Pointspass
JOHNSTON, George	21	Labourer	Scarvagh
WHITE, Samuel	26	Labourer	Newtown Hamilton
WHITE, William	32	Labourer	Newtown Hamilton
ALEXANDER, Thomas	24	Labourer	Newtown Hamilton
ALEXANDER, Sarah	20	Spinster	Newtown Hamilton
MONIGAN, William	22	Labourer	Port Norris
McQUADE, Phelemy	29	Labourer	Markethill
McQUADE, Rose	26	Spinster	Markethill
McQUADE, Bridget	20	Spinster	Markethill
McMANUS, William	26	Labourer	Moy
MAGAIN, Michael	27	Labourer	Moy
O'HANLON, Philip	24	Labourer	Moy
DICK, Samuel	27	Labourer	Scarvagh
DICK, Mary	23	Spinster	Scarvagh
SMILEY, Dominick	24	Labourer	Tanderagee
HUGHES, Patrick	26	Labourer	Tanderagee
DUNLOP, Michael	23	Labourer	Tanderagee
KEARNEY, Larry	34	Labourer	Hamilton Bawn
KEARNEY, Mary	30	Spinster	Hamilton Bawn
MORGAN, James	21	Labourer	Hamilton Bawn
RYAN, Michael	20	Labourer	Moy
McDONALD, Thomas	40	Labourer	Portadown
McDONALD, William	20	Labourer	Portadown
SURNAMAN, Thomas	36	Labourer	Clones
SPROUT, William	36	Labourer	Clones

| SHIP: | AMERICAN | | TO: | New York |
| SAIL DATE: | 25 February 1806 | | FROM: | Belfast |

NAME	AGE	OCCUPATION	RESIDENCE
BURN, Thomas	20	Labourer	Dromore
McFARNAN, Robert	21	Farmer	Dungannon
McLAUGHLIN, Malcolm	25	Labourer	Brougshane
McLAUGHLIN, Martha	19		Brougshane
McKEONN, Daniel	22		Antrim
SEEDS, James	23	Farmer	Lisburn
McGOWAN, John	22	Farmer	Armagh
McGOWAN, Margaret	23	Farmer	Armagh
CARLISLE, William	49	Farmer	Malone
CARLISLE, Mary	31	Farmer	Malone
CARLISLE, William	20	Farmer	Malone
CARLISLE, George	15	Farmer	Malone
McHAIG, John	20	Farmer	Comber
BIGAIN, William	21	Clerk	Coleraine
GRAHAM, John	27	Farmer	Lurgan
DIRINGTON, Thomas	45	Farmer	Hillsborough
BALWILL, John	25	Farmer	Larne
MACKEY, Samuel	35	Farmer	Antrim
ALLEN, Patrick	20	Farmer	Dromore
CRAIG, Samuel	21	Labourer	Larne
HYNDMAN, Hugh	27	Labourer	Antrim
JOHNSTON, Thomas	35	Labourer	Ballymoney
CAMPBELL, James	24	Farmer	Antrim
THOMSON, Robert	35	Farmer	Bangor
PATTERSON, Alexander	32	Labourer	Randlestown
ALLEN, John	37	Farmer	Lisburn
SMITH, Hugh	45	Farmer	Newtownards
BROWN, Samuel	39	Farmer	Ballymacarrick
HOLMES, Robert	27	Labourer	Crumlin
JOHNSTON, James	31	Farmer	Glenavy
JOHNSTON, Bridget	30	Farmer	Glenavy
JAMESON, William	27	Labourer	Loughbricklane
McNATTY, Hugh	34	Farmer	Bangor
BLACK, Edward	43	Farmer	Coleraine
DAVIDSON, William	29	Labourer	Dromore
BEARNS, Henry		Master	
WOOLEY, Robert		Chief Mate	
CAMPBELL, Daniel		Second Mate	
CARLISLE, James		Steward	
RYAN, Joseph		Cook	
WINGER, John		Seaman	
ROBERTS, John		Seaman	
BOYD, William		Seaman	
McGILLIGAN, John		Seaman	
ELLISON, William		Seaman	
ROGAN, Thomas		Seaman	
SMITH, James		Seaman	

SHIP:	ELIZA		TO: Baltimore
SAIL DATE:	25 February 1806		FROM: Londonderry

NAME	AGE	OCCUPATION	RESIDENCE
SNOW, Jethrow	18	Mate	Massiachasitts
SMYTH, Charles	66	Seaman	Baltimore
MURRAY, Robert	27	Seaman	Maryland
FOSTER, William	26	Seaman	Rhode Island
CLARK, J	24	Seaman	Baltimore
COOPER, Biggs	19	Seaman	Maryland
OTTEST, Margo	42	Seaman	Denmark
ROMINS, Nicholas	24	Seaman	Sweden
SLAPIT, Samuel	22	Seaman	Sweden
RILLY, Thomas	14	Apprentice	Maryland
CYRUS,	11	Apprentice	Maryland
McKINNA, Elinor	35	Spinster	Carryart
McKINNA, Eliza	14	Spinster	Carryart
McKINNA, Sarah	12	Spinster	Carryart
McKINNA, Francis	10	Boy	Carryart
McKINNA, William	7	Boy	Carryart
McKINNA, Robert	3	Boy	Carryart
MAYNE, Thomas	22	Farmer	Fintona
REA, Mathew	29	Farmer	Ramilton
SCOTT, William	18	Farmer	Ramilton
CARPENTER, Alexander	22	Farmer	Ramilton
ELDER, John	20	Farmer	Portstewart
ELDER, Stewart	18	Farmer	Portstewart
STEVENSON, Vivian	18	Farmer	Portstewart
DONNELL, John	26	Labourer	Letterkenny
ROBERT, George	19	Clerk	Newton L Vady
THOMPSON, Jane	35	Spinster	Newton L Vady
THOMPSON, James	16	Clerk	Newton L Vady
THOMPSON, Mary	14	Spinster	N L Vady
THOMPSON, Rose	12	Spinster	N L Vady
THOMPSON, Martha	10	Girl	N L Vady
THOMPSON, Margaret	8	Girl	N L Vady
McKANE, John	22	Farmer	Coleraine
McCONNELL, Alexander	19	Farmer	Ballymonne
GILBRAITH, John	22	Farmer	Samullin, Co Tyrone
GILCHRIST, M	22	Clerk	Coleraine
McGILL, Thomas	25	Merchant	St Johnston
STEWART, William	23	Clerk	N Stewart
BALLINTINE, Thomas	24	Labourer	N Stewart
BROWNE, Thomas	26	Labourer	Ballytallin
GRIFFIN, Thomas	20	Labourer	Mount Charles
McFARLAND, Robert	22	Farmer	Ballykilly
EVITT, Ann	32	Spinster	Daisyhill
EVITT, Jane	5	Girl	Daisyhill
EVITT, Elizabeth	3	Girl	Daisyhill
McCALLION, Nancy	25	Spinster	Fahan
McFARLAND, John	24	Labourer	Moy
McFARLAND, Elizabeth	20	Spinster	Moy
McFARLAND, Sarah	3	Child	Moy
McFARLAND, Jane	1	Child	Moy
IRVINE, James	7	Labourer	Moy
PIKE, William	23	Clerk	N L Vady
McCRACHAN, Hugh	20	Farmer	N L Vady
SIMPLE, Samuel	21	Farmer	Glinlush
FINLAY, William	24	Labourer	Tullywhiky
THOMPSON, James	24	Labourer	Co Derry
HANNA, John	21	Clerk	Donegal
McDERMOTT, Henry	27	Labourer	Omagh
MOSES, Bryan	26	Labourer	Omagh

SHIP:	ELIZA		TO:	Baltimore
SAIL DATE:	25 February 1806		FROM:	Londonderry

NAME	AGE	OCCUPATION	RESIDENCE
MOSES, Rose	28	Spinster	Omagh
SPROUL, Mary	40	Spinster	Omagh
SPROUL, Jane	18	Spinster	Omagh
ALCORN, William	27	Farmer	Omagh
ROGERS, Elizabeth	22	Spinster	Omagh
ANDERSON, Mary	16	Spinster	Omagh
MOSES, Charles	30	Trader	Omagh
HENRY, James	24	Labourer	N L Vady
BUCHANON, Robert	35	Merchant	America

SHIP:	GEORGE		TO:	New York
SAIL DATE:	4 March 1806		FROM:	Newry

NAME	AGE	OCCUPATION	RESIDENCE
DUFFY, Philip	45	Farmer	Monaghan
Wife to above	42		
DUFFY, Peter	28	Farmer	Monaghan
DUFFY, Michael	26	Farmer	Monaghan
DUFFY, Philip	24	Farmer	Monaghan
Wife to above	24		
DUFFY, Alice	18	Spinster	Monaghan
DUFFY, Rose	16	Spinster	Monaghan
DUFFY, Jane	14	Spinster	Monaghan
BRACIAN, James	22	Labourer	Monaghan
CONLON, Silvester	24	Farmer	Monaghan
McCRAIGH, Patrick	26	Labourer	Monaghan
Wife to above	22		
MONAGHAN, Edward	17	Labourer	Monaghan
COBURN, Robert	24	Farmer	Monaghan
Wife to above	24		
COBURN, Samuel	28	Farmer	Monaghan
McCLANCEY, Isaac	22	Labourer	Monaghan
McMEEHAN, William	26	Labourer	Monaghan
DUFFY, Thomas	24	Labourer	Monaghan
MURRY, Mary	21	Spinster	Monaghan
COBURN, Thomas	23	Labourer	Monaghan
DALEY, Pat	28	Labourer	Monaghan
Wife to above	26		
DALEY, Jane	6		
DONALDSON, John	32	Farmer	Cavan
Wife to above	30		
DONALDSON, Samuel	28	Labourer	Cavan
DONALDSON, Jane	6		
McCARNEE, William	38	Labourer	Cavan
Wife to above	30		
McCARNEE, Jane	18	Spinster	Cavan
CUNINGHAM, James	23	Labourer	Cavan
HANSHAW, Jacob		Mate	
GIFFORD, James		Seaman	
DREW, Philop		Seaman	
WYE, Stephen		Seaman	
TITUS, Eran		Seaman	
EASTON, Charles		Seaman	
NICHOLS, Edward		Cook	

NAME	AGE	OCCUPATION	RESIDENCE
BURK, Martin (Mr)	21	Merchant	Dublin
CUTHBERT, Anthony (Mr)	20	Merchant	Philadelphia
RICE, M (Mrs)	28	Gentlewoman	Dublin
HIGGINS, Francis (Mr)	40	Merchant	Philadelphia
DUNN, Ann (Mrs)	27	Spinster	Dublin
HARDIGAN, Mark (Mr)	28	Labourer	Sligo
FITZHENRY, Pat	19	Labourer	Wexford
WHELAN, Mary	20	Spinster	Wexford
SENNOTT, Miles	21	Labourer	Wexford
SMITH, Hugh	32	Labourer	Co Fermanagh
SMITH, John	21	Labourer	Co Cavan
CONNOR, Timothy	25	Labourer	Co Kildare
McGINNESS, John	14	Boy	Dublin
CLARKE, Michael	23	Book Binder	Dublin
FARRIS, Thomas	20	Labourer	Co Kildare
RINNEY, Nicholas	27	Wheelwright	Dublin
STONE, Kitty	17	Spinster	Dublin
LENNAN, Michael	19	Labourer	Kildare Town
KERNAN, James	16	Apprentice	Co Wexford
MAIN, Thomas	22	Merchant	Co Tyrone
ADAMS, Maurice	22	Mate	Philadelphia
HARP, David	24	Seaman	Delaware
CLAROON, Edward	25	Seaman	Pensylvania
RODGERS, Henry	25	Seaman	Norfolk, Virginia
HALL, Jehroe	35	Cook	Delaware
WILLIAMS, John	24	Stewart	Charlestown
HAYDTRAIN, Guslavus	32	Seaman	Wesmare, Sweden
HANLOW, George	24	Seaman	Delaware
HUTCHINGS, William	23	Seaman	Philadelphia
DOWSE, Edward	14	Apprentice	Dublin
SAWYER, Abel	16	Seaman	Portland, Massachusetts

SHIP:	AUGUSTA			TO: New York
SAIL DATE:	11 March 1806			FROM: Dublin

NAME	AGE	OCCUPATION	RESIDENCE
EGERTON, William	9	Child	Street, Meath
EGERTON, John	11	Child	Street, Meath
COUGHEN, Peggy	50	Married	Ballyfinn, Queens County
COUGHEN, Phanton	15	Labourer	Ballyfinn, Queens County
COUGHEN, William	13	Child	Ballyfinn, Queens County
COUGHEN, Catherine	11	Child	Ballyfinn, Queens County
COUGHEN, Biddy	9	Child	Ballyfinn, Queens County
COUGHEN, Nathanial	8	Child	Ballyfinn, Queens County
COUGHEN, Jolind	7	Child	Ballyfinn, Queens County
COUGHEN, Balt	6	Child	Ballyfinn, Queens County
WATERS, William	25	Labourer	Navan, Queens County
CROSSBRETH, Patrick	22	Labourer	Ballyfinn, Queens County
CONNOR, Margaret	19	Spinster	Waterford,
JACKSON, John	24	Merchant	America
CROFTS, Alexander	24	Merchant	Dublin
TURBROTHER, John	29	Clerk	Dublin
CHARLETON, Ralph	28	Merchant	America
SCALLION, James	40	Gentleman	America
EATON, James	23	Clerk	Waterford
EATON, Ellen	18	Spinster	Waterford
O'CONNOR, John		Master	
ELPLIN, Micheal		Mate	
WARLOW, Benjamin		Sailor	
WILSON, James		Sailor	
HELTON, John		Sailor	
ABRAHANS, John		Sailor	
CROWDER, Robert		Sailor	
MEEHAN, Michael		Sailor	
JENKINS, Benjamin		Sailor	
DIXON, James		Sailor	
DOOLEY, James		Sailor	
BOOBY, Vale		Sailor	

SHIP:	WESTPOINT		TO: New York
SAIL DATE:	11 March 1806		FROM: Londonderry

NAME	AGE	OCCUPATION	RESIDENCE
UPDIKE, Daniel	32	Mate	New York
DENNISON, William	34	Second Mate	New York
NESBITT, Robert	22	Seaman	New York
WARD, John	29	Seaman	New York
ALDERIDGE, George	18	Seaman	New York
CUNNINGHAM, Nat	16	Seaman	New York
SPINGER, Fred	24	Seaman	New York
McLOUGHLIN, Jason	24	Seaman	New York
BEGLEY, Jason	24	Seaman	New York
WHEELEN, Martin	27	Seaman	New York
WILIAMS, John	31	Steward	New York
PEARCE, John	30	Cook	New York
BROWN, Nathan	25	Seaman	New York
HEMPTON, James	15	Apprentice	New York
KERR, William	26	Farmer	Enniskillen
KERR, Peggy	26	Spinster	Enniskillen
KERR, Robert	4	Boy	Enniskillen
BRACKEN, Jason	18	Farmer	Enniskillen
BRACKEN, John	24	Farmer	Enniskillen
BRACKEN, Margaret	23	Spinster	Enniskillen
FULLON, John	25	Farmer	Agivy
WARD, Thomas	29	Farmer	Glenward
WARD, Nelly	28	Spinster	Glenward
WARD, Charles	5	Child	Glenward
CRAWFORD, Robert	18	Farmer	Near Castlefin
ROULSTON, James	22	Farmer	Near Castlefin
CAMPBELL, Ann	36	Spinster	Dungiven
CAMPBELL, Letitia	6¹/₂	Child	Dungiven
FORSTER, Thomas	29	Farmer	Co Fermanagh
FORSTER, Elleanor	25	Spinster	Co Fermanagh
KNOX, William	22	Clerk	Ballysheagh
HALL, Samuel	22	Clerk	Conohan
GILL, Sarah	20	Spinster	Edinburagh
WILSON, Mathew	19	Clerk	Maughrabau
KENNEDY, Henry	24	Labourer	Mount Charles
FREEBORN, Thomas	31	Labourer	Ballyshannon
HAMILTON, William	23	Farmer	Ballyshannon
HAMILTON, Ann	20	Spinster	Ballyshannon
KIRKPATRICK, William	20	Farmer	Drumholm
MOBAY, Philip	22	Farmer	Drumholm
REED, James	20	Farmer	Drumholm
HETHERINGTON, Jason	22	Farmer	Drumholm
KEYS, George	25	Farmer	Drumholm
KEYS, Jane	26	Spinster	Drumholm
FENSTON, Thomas	28	Farmer	Drumholm
THOMPSON, Jason	32	Farmer	Drumholm
THOMPSON, Rebecca	20	Spinster	Drumholm
THOMPSON, Crissy	8	Girl	Drumholm
THOMPSON, Catherine	6	Child	Drumholm
DONNELL, Andrew	19	Labourer	Drumholm
DUNLIAVY, Mary	21	Spinster	Drumholm
MILLAR, Hugh	20	Farmer	Donegal
BEATTY, John	19	Labourer	Meaghera
McQUILLON, James	19	Labourer	Agivy
McALICE, James	21	Labourer	Agivy
McGARVEY, Patrick	19	Laborer	Kilmacrenan
LAMBERT, Robert	26	Farmer	Castledawson
LENNAN, Edward	28	Labourer	Castledawson
CRAIG, James	27	Farmer	Castlefin

SHIP:	WESTPOINT		TO:	New York
SAIL DATE:	11 March 1806		FROM:	Londonderry

NAME	AGE	OCCUPATION	RESIDENCE
BARR, Samuel	18	Farmer	Castlefin
THOMPSON, Ann	23	Spinster	Derry
O'BRIEN, ?	33	Spinster	Derry
WILSON, John	23	Farmer	Strarodden
ARMSTRONG, Christopher	22	Farmer	Irvinestown
GINN, James	23	Farmer	Irvinestown
GINN, Arthur	6	Boy	Irvinestown
ADAMS, William	18	Labourer	Glenstall
CROCKET, David	23	Farmer	Drumnashiel
?, Stewart	18	Farmer	Rohan
BARRY, Sarah	52	Spinster	Derry
BARRY, Eleanor	28	Spinster	Derry
BARRY, Ann	9	Spinster	Derry
GOORLEY, Eliza	18	Servant	Derry
DERMOTT, Andrew	20	Servant	Derry
KERR, Ann	3	Child	Enniskillen
BRACKEN, Robert	3	Child	Enniskillen
BRACKEN, John	2	Child	Enniskillen
THOMPSON, Sarah	1	Child	Drumholm
THOMPSON, Isaac	2	Child	Drumholm
BRITTON, William	16	Farmer	Donegal
DOGHERTY, James	20	Labourer	Ramelton
McCABE, Robert	30	Farmer	Co Armagh
McLAUGHLIN, Wm	22		Derryvain
BRADLEY, John	19	Labourer	Muff
JACKSON, Hugh	21	Farmer	Castlefin
JAIMSON, Alex	19	Farmer	Castlefin
JAIMSON, Henry	35	Farmer	Castlefin
JAIMSON, James	27	Farmer	Castlefin
MURPHY, William	19	Farmer	Castlefin

INDEX

INDEX

INDEX

129

INDEX

INDEX

INDEX

INDEX

FREIL	Thomas	81	GARVEY	John	116	GILMOR	James	54
FRENCH	Shepherd	29	GAULT	Samuel	66		Jourdan	54
FRESCHMOLLER	Hanibal	57	GAVAN	John	33		Rose	54
FRONLER	Thomas	72	GEERN	Fleury	65		William	54
FULD	Alexander	52	GERAHTY	Martin	113	GILMORE	Jane	54
FULHAM	Arthur	30		Nancy	113	GILMOUR	Ann	9
FULLARD	Eliza	48	GETTY	Abigail	61		Samuel	9
	Frances	48		James	61	GINN	Anne	63
	Jane	48		John	61		Arthur	125
FULLERTON	Agnes	96	GIBSON	Ann	50		James	125
	James	49		Charles W	116		Jane	63
FULLON	John	124		David	50		John	63
FULTON	Alexander	34		Eliza	63		Margaret	63
	James	42		Elizabeth	50	GITTEN	Child	41
	James	60		Elizabeth	84		John	41
	James	80		Fanny	63	GLASEY	William	99
	James	88		Frances	95	GLEN	Jannet	106
	Mary	88		Francis	95		Jean	106
	Nancy	43		John	20		Jeany	106
	Robert	43		John	50		Margaret	106
	Thomas	80		John	63		Samuel	106
	Thomas	109		John	84		Wm	106
GABBY	Hugh	34		Mary	50	GLENNING	Mary	48
GALBRAITH	James	57		Mathew	63		Patrick	48
GALE	Henry	107		Robert	1	GLIN	William	14
GALLAGHER	Edward	88		Robert	50	GOLDEN	Michael	44
	Hugh	90		Samuel	95	GONAGLE	Peter	17
	John	65		Sarah	50	GONELL	William	81
	Mary	63		William	97	GOODMAN	Miles	80
	Owen	88	GIDDIE	James	86	GOODWIN	Randolph	99
	Patrick	65	GIFFORD	Andrew	72	GOOEY	Robert	7
	Simon Felix	30		James	121	GOORLEY	Eliza	125
GALLAUGHER	John	11	GILAN	Pat	6	GORDON	Elizabeth	111
GALLIER	Elizabeth	90	GILBRAITH	John	119		George	101
	William	90	GILCHRIST	M	119		James	46
GALLON	David	5	GILFEADER	Edmond	17		John	55
GALWAY	James	24	GILL	Roger	44		John	91
GAMBLE	Edward	90		Sarah	124		Margaret	42
	James	63	GILLAN	James	6		Miss	53
	Robert	96	GILLESPIE	Alexander	74		Thomas	42
GANET	James	34		Hugh	74		Thomas	111
GARDEN	William	88		James	90	GORE	James	41
GARDINER	John	99		Margaret	74		James	48
GARDNER	Alish	74		Neil	85	GORMAN	Edward	53
	Singleton	74	GILLESPY	Jane	103		John	86
	Thomas	74		Patt	68		Thomas	46
GARRET	James	28		Peggy	68		William	69
GARRETT	Henry	24	GILMARTIN	Daniel	6	GORMERS	John	65
	S Ann	24		Daniel	17	GOTHAN	William	53
GARRIGLE	Michael	112		Pat	6	GOURLEY	Jane	71
GARTER	Owen	53	GILMOR	Frances	54		William	71

136

INDEX

138

INDEX

INDEX

INDEX

INDEX

INDEX

INDEX

INDEX

INDEX

INDEX

153

INDEX